George Alfred Lawrence

Silverland

George Alfred Lawrence

Silverland

ISBN/EAN: 9783743322257

Manufactured in Europe, USA, Canada, Australia, Japa

Cover: Foto ©Thomas Meinert / pixelio.de

Manufactured and distributed by brebook publishing software (www.brebook.com)

George Alfred Lawrence

Silverland

SILVERLAND.

SILVERLAND.

BY THE

AUTHOR OF "GUY LIVINGSTONE," &c.

Difficile est, propriè communia dicere.

LONDON:
CHAPMAN AND HALL, 193, PICCADILLY.
1873.

SILVERLAND.

CHAPTER I.

On a certain afternoon in last October, we drove seawards over the Cornish uplands. It was the seventh day of the week, and over all things there brooded a very Sabbath calm; we were out of ear-shot of the stream-ripples in the dell; even the leaves were silent in the covert-belt where we sprung the first woodcock of the season yester-even; there was never a wave or rustle in the ferns and grasses fringing the high field-banks; and the air was still as a dream.

Ere long, the silence was troubled with a sound, vague and faint from distance at first, but waxing in volume and distinctness, till it might be likened to the beat of a mighty drum, heavily muffled—such an one as used to be smitten long ago in the courtyard of the Great Khan when the battalia of Tartary was set in array. Said my companion, answering the question of my eyes,—

"The ground-sea is on to-day. There will be trouble with the nets, before morning."

I did not wonder that he said it gravely; for, as the hop-bins are to those whose ensign is the White Horse of Hengist, and the wine-vats to the Rhinelander, so are the pilchard-seines to every true Cornishman bred and born within hail of the coast.

Soon, we came to a narrow gorge, trending shore-wards so steeply, that at sight thereof an up-country horse might have sweated from fear; but our hardy moorland galloway scuttled down it without breaking his trot, till we halted on the wide stretch of ribbed brown sand underlying the cliff-walls. A sight awaited us there—to me, at least, wonderful and strange.

On the ocean—we were looking over the Atlantic, remember, with never a rock or islet nearer than Cape Race—there was no more sign of storm than in the air; for the sullen heave and welter in the offing was not discernible from where we stood. Only two or three thin white lines of foam, following each other regularly, showed that there was stir in the waters where they began to shoal: but each great billow, on reaching a certain point, upheaved itself with a motion, slow and solemn, yet inexpressibly suggestive of strength, till it was reared like a wall betwixt us and the low westering sun; and then, curving ponderously, fell with a dead massive shock, that seemed to make the very sands shake and quiver. And the sound. Well—I have listened to many voices of the sea; to the hiss of the under-tow, ravaging pebble ridges; to the rattle of the surf, grinding great boulders as the mill grinds corn; to the crash of waves repulsed from granite bulwarks; to the thunder of billows, penetrating into the bowels of the land through caverns that have never seen the sun: but, before or since, I have heard nothing like this sombre monotone.

After a while, we considered what manner of turmoil it must have been in mid-ocean, of which those rollers were but the faint outward ripple; and, speaking of the humours of the Atlantic, I called to mind a certain storm wherein I was buffeted some eight years agone—the storm that proved the sea-worthiness of the Monitors, off Cape

Hatteras, with fatal issue. And so we fell to talking of men and scenes, encountered in that same luckless journey; and to my comrade's question, "Would you like to see them all again?" I made answer, carelessly, as one is wont to speak of any scheme utterly vague and impracticable,—

"I should like it of all things."

The subject dropped then; and, during a fortnight of better wild shooting than has often fallen to my lot, it was not again recurred to. Turnips thrive right well on the light upland soil; and the birds—plentiful enough for reasonable desires—will actually lie, even in late October, to steady setters; furthermore, snipe and fowl are not among the myths of North Cornwall. Therefore, as you may guess, I carried away grateful memories when I set my face eastwards: but the memory of those words spoken on the sea-shore, was not among them. I was much taken aback when, in the January ensuing, my host appeared before me, and quoth he,—

"Have you forgotten what you said, that Sunday afternoon down in Trevenna Cove? I must start within a fortnight for the West—for the very far West. Am I to go alone?"

Albeit I fully endorsed his purpose when I heard the nature of his errand, I fell into a great perplexity. Travel across the Atlantic and the Rocky Mountains in mid-winter, with all possible advantages of convoy thrown in, is not tempting; and, under ordinary circumstances, I should surely have declined with thanks, and without parley. But there are comrades—and comrades—you see; and, since the worthies who went out with Pendragon to war, I think there has not breathed stauncher backer, in field, feast, or fray, than he who stood looking on me, then, with wistful eyes.

So I said I would think about it.

Now most men—and many women, for the matter of that—know what such a concession comes to. Thus it befell that, on about the sunniest morning of a darksome January, Tressilian and I—his is a name of travel, of course—stood on the deck of the good ship 'China,' outward bound.

Fair weather kept us company all down the Channel; and we made such good way, that, rounding Roche's Point early in the forenoon, we were forced to anchor for some hours, waiting the mails. The tardy steam-tug took us on shore, too late to visit any of the beauties of the harbour. There is nothing to see, immediately around the railway station; and we saw it thoroughly. Some half-dozen passengers — full of wassail, as it seemed, though the day was yet young —drove up and down on low-backed cars, out-yelling their charioteers. Watching such enthusiasts, you begin to understand, how the swings and merry-go-rounds at fairs and races are filled. Eight years had brought no changes to the dull squalid landing-place; there was the same beggar with his hoarse blessings, ten for sixpence, that sounded so like malisons,—the same harridan, proffering sickly shamrocks,—the same *colleen*, with dusky elf-locks, and broad blue eyes *à fleur de tête*, cackling treasonable ditties in a subdued treble, as though in fear of instant arrest; albeit she is probably subsidised by our indulgent rulers, to ensure the emigrant's latest sniff of Irish air having a flavour of faction. The farce does not repay a second visit; and we were well content to set foot on the 'China' once more.

The clouds began to bank up as we weighed anchor, and there was menace of foul weather in the watery moon. Before we passed Cape Clear, the good ship had given us a foretaste of the 'lively' qualities for which she is renowned; and, when dawn broke on the morrow, a sullen grey sky brooded over a leaden sea.

My experience of nausea is entirely vicarious; nevertheless, I am acquainted with no such detestable winter quarters as the mid-Atlantic. There, you soon realise that 'unrest in rest' is not such a paradox after all. Without any pretence to seamanship, there are many who feel a kind of personal interest in a battle with winds and waves, under sail; but you can hardly throw your heart into the efforts of mere machinery. The log—supposing you have no bets on the result—resolves itself into a question of knots and hours: if the ship has made extra good time, she has done her duty—no more; if otherwise, the British grumbler, keeping well out of earshot of the Captain, asserts himself very freely. An ungracious, unchristian frame of mind; but what would you have? The struggle with garments and bath, attending each rising up and lying down,—the struggle over meals, when the dishes, despite their leading-strings, tumble about in an idiotic infantile fashion,—the struggle with an atmosphere innocent of fresh air, and laden with the stale odours of baked meats,—the struggle with the sloping slippery deck, when you make a pretence of taking exercise,—the eternal tremor and grind of the screw, that seems to vibrate through nerves and brain at last; all these minor miseries make up rather a high trial of the 'old Adam.' A practical divine, I believe, once estimated that "an even temper was worth 500*l.* a year." According to this tariff, and from this source alone, Tressilian's income ought to be about 2000*l.*, paid quarterly. But even he succumbed to the malign influences, ere long, in the form of a mild melancholy, which would have been quite touching, if one had had any compassion to spare.

The monotony of 'strong head winds from the west' may, occasionally, be broken by a real tempest; and this diversion we did not lack. On the sixth forenoon, during a treacherous gleam of sunshine, the mercury began to fall, faster than it had ever done during our captain's long experience of these seas.

> Then, with a sudden flaw,
> Round veered the gusty skaw;

and, at nightfall, we were running at full steam-power, and with every stitch of canvas set that could safely be carried, before a furious south-easterly gale. The deck being impossible, and the saloon intolerable, I was 'bouning myself to rest,' seated on our scanty couch, when there came a lurch of lurches. At the moment, I was about as helpless as Agamemnon when he was stricken by the felon blow—being indeed entangled ἐνι χίτωνι; and, being hurled bodily across the cabin, I was only brought up by the woodwork of the opposite berth, with 'serious damage to figure-head.' An hour later—lying swathed in wet bandages, stupid, and still half stunned—I was aware of a shock, a crash, and a quiver of the ship from stern to stem; and my servant, entering hastily, told us that "the saloon was knee-deep in water." Since, some years ago, he first followed my fortunes, I had not seen his sedate countenance seriously perturbed; and, with a certain satisfaction, I now noted a ruffling of its serenity. Though we were going all sixteen knots, one of the billows ravening in our track had got more way on yet; and, tumbling inboard over the quarter, stormed the saloon through a shattered panel; crushing in the roof of the wheel-house to boot, and knocking a quartermaster or so completely out of time. However, the gale, as if satisfied with having proved its power, began thenceforth to abate; and, though we never saw the sun, or rode on a level keel, till we had left the Newfoundland banks far behind, the Atlantic refrained from further violence.

Our fellow-voyagers were a very level lot: the commercial element, of course, largely predominating; for few, at this season, travel for their pleasure. Yet we made some pleasant acquaintances—notably that of an American ex-minister, who, in long sojourn in the sunny South, had nearly lost his nationality. The slow soft voice, languid gentleness of manner, and thorough *insouciance*, savoured far more of Castile than Kentucky. Also, he had lived in close intimacy with the luckless Maximilian; and, though loth to broach the subject, he told us enough to revive regrets for as good and gallant a gentleman as any that have died *für Ehr und Recht*.

The passenger-list held another name, known to all who have perused a certain famous 'Diary.' Here was the irrepressible Wigfall—whilome Confederate senator and general; now, as a sardonic Yankee put it, "loafing around on the mining tack;" but still

Impiger, iracundus, inexorabilis, acer,

as when he bearded our Arch-Special under Fort Sumter's guns. This 'outrage,' perchance, brought him evil luck; for the world seems to have gone hardly with him since, and amongst his own countrymen he had little honour. Some of these last looked on that inroad of the sea as a kind of judgment on his rebel talk, that then chanced to be in full swing. Nevertheless, an honest heart, I warrant it; and none of us Britishers wished him other than good speed down in Colorado.

At the close of Atlantic voyages, certain ceremonials are seldom omitted, unless from stress of weather. All these were duly performed,—the chorus-singing—the mock trial (the criminal was represented by an 'Israelite indeed,' the like of whom I have not seen off the stage)—the lottery of the pilot-boat's number—the vote of thanks and confidence to the Captain; albeit this last was more than a mere formality. Early on the fourteenth morning we sighted Sandy Hook.

CHAPTER II.

The low shores were deeply fringed with snow and rime; the bare branches on the ridge of Staten Island stood out sharp against a steel-blue sky; and, crossing the New Jersey ferry, we encountered more than one ice-floe driving seaward from the Hudson. Thus, we began to realise that there might be germs of truth in those rumours of trouble in the far West which, on the landing stage in the Mersey, sounded like idle words; and these misgivings were strengthened that same evening.

We were scarcely housed at 'The Brevoort,'—cosy, and full of Apician appliances as of old,—when two or three of the kindly folk, for whom we brought letters, came to make us welcome. From these we learned that, for fully three weeks, no pioneers had been found strong or bold enough to force the entrenchments within which the Erl King held his own against all comers, laying embargo even on the mails. The limits of the blockade were ill defined: men spoke of it vaguely as stretching westwards from Cheyenne—the most formidable obstacles lying along the Laramie plains, and on the slopes of the Wahsatch range. Provoking news, certainly, for those who were bound to press forward; yet the enforced delay lacked not solace.

I think, one ought to be unfettered by any business or mission, to thoroughly appreciate the hospitalities of the Empire City. It is so pleasant to believe, that there is nothing venal or official in the frank and free courtesies proffered at every turn. I do not speak of banquetings and junketings alone; though a dinner at the Manhattan Club, prepared by an artist whose salary might have lured Ude across the Atlantic—were that Chief still in the flesh—is a joy to be remembered; but of the consideration and indulgence shown even to the prejudices of the stranger.

This, remember, was an exceptional time. The controversy concerning the Alabama claims was in its first bitterness; the ultra-Republican press teemed with warlike leaders; and the sporting editor of the *Herald* had backed up his sensationals with a wager of 3000 to 2000 dollars on cartels being exchanged with England within six short weeks. Nevertheless, in not one of the clubs whereof we were incontinently made free—in not one of the houses in which we were made welcome, —did we hear aught to disquiet the most patriotic Britisher; and we all know with what promptitude, especially when on foreign soil, *acuit sua cornua Taurus.* And we communed with lawyers, whose opinions carry weight, not in the courts alone; with senators, who seldom lack heedful audiences when they catch the Vice-President's eye; with soldiers, whose renown dates back beyond the civil war; and with more than one editor, never suspected of Anglican proclivities. Furthermore, Tressilian, in his legislative capacity, was a tempting mark for argument.

That cloud has happily vanished, like others that seemed pregnant with storm; but, if the tempest had broken loose—setting commercial interests wholly aside—I verily believe there would have been heaviness at more true and wise hearts on that side of the Atlantic than on ours.

It is unfair to read the American aristocracy—using the word in its original, not in its applied and conventional sense—by the light of journalism or platform-oratory; especially on the verge of a General Election. And even for the 'tall talk' there is some excuse, when you remember what an infinite variety of personal interests are at stake. Perhaps, the candidates for the Presidency themselves are not more keenly alive to the result, than the postmaster of Muddy Creek, or the collector at Poverty Flat. Like the ring in the wedding-cake, the omnipotent 'dollar' lies at the core of almost every *caucus* and convention. 'Needs must when the devil drives,' applies not to Transatlantic politicians alone; and, at such a season, Mammon bestirs himself with a will.

A very brief stay in New York will convince you that the temptations to money-making must be quite as strong as when—*Rectè si possis*—was penned. Paris, Naples, and Vienna would hardly be selected for purposes of retrenchment; but, in comparison of costliness, the Empire City wins, with something in hand. It needs time, experience, and ingenuity to procure any article, necessary or superfluous, at a moderate price; excepting, perhaps, oysters, apples, and seats in street-cars. But these edibles alone will not satisfy all constitutions; and, if a man could lodge on the tramways, he must still be clothed in civilized fashion. The tariff at some hotels and boarding-houses does not sound so exorbitant; but liquors rule fabulously high; and 'quenchers,' at fifty cents, will tell at the year's end. After careful calculation, you realise that a dollar about represents an English shilling—rather an upsetting of one's ideas of exchange.

At every turn, you meet evidences of overweening wealth and luxury. Taking up the 'Ledger'—a serious journal, specially adapted for the perusal of families and schools—you find its proprietor proffering sums that might have bought Favonius, before a leaf dropped from his chaplet, for any trotter that can beat Dexter's time; and this is no gambler, remember, but a decent 'sponsible burgess, setting his face against public matches and wagering like a very flintstone. Calling in Fifth Avenue, you learn that the morning dress, that does ample justice to the *svelte* figure, is fresh from the Rue de la Paix; and that your hostess "thinks it almost the cheapest plan, on the whole." Fancy an economy, with Worth as its fountain-head! Dining at Delmonico's —excellent well, no doubt—if allowed a glimpse of the bill, you will find your share of meat, drink, and tobacco amount to about eight sovereigns sterling. For the transit from the club to your hotel—a brief bowshot for a practised archer—whilst the night is yet young, your hackman demands a couple of dollars or so, without a shade of compunction on his ignoble face, or a twinkle of mirth in his lowering eyes. [Parenthetically, I wish someone, well versed in acclimatisation, would explain why the Irish car-driver, who had ever a jest—albeit somewhat mild and stale—on his lips, and would liever have earned a crown at a meet of the 'Ward' than a pound-note at a prayer-meeting, is transformed, by a few gulps of American air, into a covetous, sullen savage, with rather less notion of humour or amenity than attaches to his Parisian compeer.] If you 'plunge' at all in gloves, on the Jerome Park, or other race-track, and the good things come off wrong, you will find your account not much easier to settle than after a disastrous Newmarket meeting.

To be sure, the money that circulates so rapidly is oft-times lightly won; for the audacity of our 'bulls' and 'bears' pales before the ordinary operations of Wall Street—not taking into account such crises as the Black Friday, or the recent conflict over

Erie's. I doubt if the financial history of the world can match, at least in rapidity and subtlety of construction, the stupendous fortune now owned by Vanderbilt, of whom more hereafter. But—taking all in—New York, enticing as it may be for brief sojourn, is scarcely the abiding-place for a pauper troubled with a conscience.

The papers, at that time, were still redolent of the Fisk tragedy ; indeed, scarce a day passed without a legal wrangle about the assassin's impending trial. But Society seemed somewhat weary—perhaps, somewhat ashamed—of the subject ; only a very few vouchsafed contemptuous pity to the dead, such as might have been felt in old times when a knavish court-buffoon had come to a violent end.

About the City and Custom House frauds, however, and the like misdemeanors, people were thoroughly in earnest ; and the public was not apt to err on the side of clemency. At any rate, the huge mansion has a fair chance of being swept, if not garnished ; and, whilst the 'other seven' are barred out, the motley household may hope to live cleanly.

Our courteous hosts backed their invitations with warnings, against the folly of trusting to the tender mercies of the Union Pacific; and, as a purely uncommercial traveller, I was moved to tarry amongst these convivial prophets. But the chiefs of our company, in their austere virtue, decided otherwise. So, on the sixth night we set our faces towards the West.

The party had been gradually augmented, till we counted eleven in all; the latest addition being a bride, whose matronhood was not a full week old. Would even Mrs. Malaprop have approved of such a honeymoon as awaited this intrepid couple? The other notables comprised a Professor of great repute, studious and careful, yet brisk and gay of demeanour withal under each and every trial; a Senator, who, before he represented his State, had been a luminary of Western law; a Lieutenant, R.N., with whom we had formed alliance on the voyage out; and last, though certainly not least, the eminent person who for the next two months was to be our guide and guardian. Very soon, in honour of his wondrous talent as director and purveyor, he was dubbed 'Commodore;' and many titles, civil and military, on that side of the Atlantic, are less justly earned.

I once sojourned at Homburg, in a right pleasant

company, now scattered widely over the earth—and beneath it, for that matter. For first and foremost was a famous inditer of prose and rhyme; and, years ago,

Multis ille bonis flebilis, occidit.

Like most men of that grand stamp, he was merry as a school-boy in his holiday; and, wasting not his substance at the tables, was free to enjoy to the uttermost the varied entertainments. Partly in jest, partly in earnest, he was wont to avow a grateful and implicit trust in the Administration, who purveyed so liberally for their guests. One morning, a comparative stranger required his opinion as to weather prospects. Folding his hands meekly, 'with a child-like and bland-like smile,' answered the Professor,—

"I cannot say. But I shall be content with whatever my 'good gentlemen' are pleased to provide."

Into some such beatific frame of mind, before we had been long under the Commodore's tutelage, both Tressilian and I subsided; taking no more thought of the morrow, so far as transport and food were concerned, than if we had been a couple of errant sparrows. The traveller, indeed, who would grumble at a Palace Car, so conducted, had best bide at home. It is the very sublimation of the old *vetturino* system; omitting the venal element and preliminary fight over the contract.

We left the streets of New York ankle-deep in mire; but it was mid-winter again when, on the following forenoon we stood over against Niagara. A white haze, denser than the thickest spray-mist, veiling the Falls nearly to their crest, clung to the cliffs on either hand; through which, rank above rank, glimmered the giant ice-spears. The view upwards from the Suspension Bridge was somewhat blurred and dim: but there was reality enough in the awful turmoil immediately beneath it and below. The encroaching shore-ice seemed rather to provoke than allay the fury of the current, that in a few seconds ground huge bergs into clots of seething foam; and this side of the great picture was assuredly more marvellous than when I looked on it last under a July sun.

The stunted woodlands were all a-glitter, and rime lay thick on the hungry tilths, but not a deep drift appeared anywhere; and one or two of our party, arguing from the average of Canadian winters, began to hope that rumour had exaggerated the difficulties farther west. At Detroit, however, which we reached about midnight, I fancy the last of these illusions vanished.

The passage of the St. Clair river—the strait betwixt the inland seas of Huron and Erie—was decidedly sensational. By dint of incessant driving to and fro at the top of her thousand horse-power, the steam-ferry had maintained her right of way; but, before our train had been run aboard in a double section, the floes had closed in; and, as her mighty bows grided through, there arose an angry roar of tormented ice; whilst great splinters and fragments leapt up against her sides, like prairie wolves besetting a buffalo bull.

A faulty axle—the first of many such disasters—caused us to miss the Western train at Chicago; so that we were constrained to abide there the third night. The delay was easy to endure; for what we saw that afternoon was worth a greater sacrifice.

On one side of the picture was the sorry image of a fair city, lying in a ruinous heap; but on the other was such a presentment of commercial courage and energy, as, I believe, lacks parallel in this world of ours. From amongst hillocks of shivered stones, from amongst tottering walls riven and distorted by the strange fantasies of fire, from ghastly hollows of foundations laid bare, went up the diligent sound of trowel and hammer; nor was the frost, that keeps most masons at home, any hindrance to these sturdy craftsmen. We saw one six-storied block of good substantial brickwork, that was roofed within eleven weeks of the digging of its foundations. One of the proprietors of the Sherman House—a hostel which has few superiors in the West—averred to us that his old home was still blazing, when he completed the purchase of the building in which we found good entertainment; and, on the first night after the flames abated, he was able to shelter therein some three hundred homeless heads.

I was told—not by a native, but by one of the few strangers who watched Chicago throughout her terrible ordeal—that, for just one day after the actual panic had subsided, people sat down, sullenly, face to face with the utter ruin. Thenceforward, a healthy elasticity was almost universal—each man setting his hand to his appointed work, in the spirit of the steadfast Consul who 'never despaired of the Republic.' Assuredly, ere long, the Queen of the West will lift up her brow, vauntingly as heretofore; though, for years to come, it must bear seams and scars.

There was pointed out to us one strange caprice of the Destroyer. In the very centre of the quarter that suffered most severely, stands a dwelling of fair proportions, built entirely of wood, with a tiny grove around it meant rather for ornament than shelter. When the flames came near, the family fled, like their fellows; and returned, when the tyranny was overpast, to look upon the ashes of their homestead. It bore neither scorch nor scathe; the foliage of the limes was scarce more shrivelled than is usual in arid autumn; and there the house still abides—opposite a stately stone church, riven and blasted from spire to threshold,—such a wonder as, perchance, has not been matched since the time of the Three Children.

When time is of such vital importance, it is unfair to criticise too severely builders' handiwork; yet one would have thought that people, still half crushed by such a disaster, would have been more careful to avert its recurrence. If pitch and asphalte are excluded, there is still too much of flimsy brickwork, too little of iron and stone; and, were I director of an insurance office, I should not, even now, be over-anxious for business in Chicago.

The waterworks, however, which, with great damage, barely escaped ruin, have been greatly strengthened and enlarged; the supplies, drawn through a tunnel running far out into Lake Michigan, are quite inexhaustible; and, after such a warning, even supine officials are not likely to be taken unawares.

Amongst other signs of reviving commerce, is a tolerably brisk trade in relics. No stranger is suffered to depart without investing in one or more of the miniature bells made, nominally, out of the metal of that one which went on tolling in the Court House, till it was half molten. In almost every Western town and hamlet, you hear their tinkling; and the original must have multiplied itself, in the miraculous fashion of

> Peter's nose, and Bridget's toes,
> And Apollonius' hair.

Early on the morrow we embarked on the 'Arlington,' which, for the next two months, was to be more or less our home. The interior of these Palace Cars, I suppose, has been often enough described,—the saloon, bright with polished woods, gilding, and harmonious colours; opening into state rooms that you may turn into hermitages if you will,—the cosy tables, so temptingly spread at meal hours,—the compact caboose, more wonderful in its faculties of production and reproduction than any conjuror's hat,—the sleeping appliances of sliding seats and descending panels, from which arise a double tier of couches decorously curtained, more than spacious enough for the repose of ordinary mortality. But it needs long and actual experience of these institutions, to do full justice to their merits.

We were, perhaps, exceptionally favoured. Purveyors like the Commodore are rare; and one might not always find such amiable and amenable officials as the conductor of the Arlington, or waiters deft and zealous as his sable subordinates. Nevertheless 'Henry'—meekest and merriest of created beings by nature—was, when the devil of drink possessed him, too often overcome by an insane desire of 'putting a head' on the world in general, and on his coloured brethren in particular. He had repented tearfully, and, at our intercession, had been forgiven seven times at least, when the Commodore, refusing again to temper justice with mercy, left him in ward amongst the Mormons. I trust that the wife, whose letters or silence were the invariable excuse for his backslidings, has, long ere this, taken the simple sinner back to her ample bosom.

Smoothly, if not swiftly, we swept on through the rolling corn-lands of Illinois; and there first began to realise the marvels of Western agriculture. The rail traverses, we were told, one maize-plot of a thousand acres, in a ring-fence; and it was easy to believe this; for, on either hand, far beyond ken, bare stalks peered above the shallow snow. Further south in the State, there is farming on a yet more colossal scale; but we saw quite enough, to feel assured that the reports which have reached Europe fall rather short of the truth.

The price of land varies, of course, in proportion to its remoteness from town or rail—perhaps from twenty to twenty-five dollars an acre would be a fair average, after Chicago is left some score of miles behind. In Iowa—scarcely inferior in its fertile resources—prices are still more moderate. Taking this tariff, and allowing that it is worth something to abide a little while longer under the old Dominion, I admire rather the energy than the wisdom of the settler who prefers hewing his way, inch by inch, through a Canadian clearing, to the trenching of soft prairie loam, where neither stock nor stone will blunt a ploughshare. A year ago, one of our party watched an Iowa farmer breaking up virgin soil: the first furrow ran straight, for hard on a league, before the team was turned.

Crossing the Mississippi at Burlington, we rolled on, without notable let or hindrance, till Council Bluffs towered on our right. A pile-bridge, chiefly supported by Missouri ice, took us into Omaha,—a dreary depressing town enough; though, they say, its future looms large, and it can boast already of having made the fortunes of George Francis Train. Here we halted another night for repairs; and, henceforward, time-tables became things of the past.

To English ears a snow-blockade may sound a small matter, of lighter interest than a single grave casualty. Do you know what it means out here?

It means nothing less than utter stagnation of commerce, involving ruin to many, privation and distress to all—a moral twilight, during which none can commune with his fellows, save by use of the overtaxed wires, that often prove faithless to their trust. Figures in these parts are not always to be swallowed 'unsalted'; but, after careful inquiry, we could not believe that the estimate of eight million dollars, set on the merchandise locked up in this fatal spring, was much exaggerated. On the hardships, perils, and sore sickness—mortal in not a few cases—endured by those who were actually in thrall, I have not space to dwell; yet, if you had traversed a car, in which forty human beings had been cabined for over a week, with every outlet barred against the cold, cooking their scanty victuals on a couple of greasy stoves, and sleeping almost pell-mell, you might have thought this last item not the lightest in the heavy score.

And with whom is reckoning to be made?

The scope of Western malison is so extensive, that it may be doubted if the Directors of the Union Pacific have deserved *all* the strong language levelled at them of late. There is, of course, the excuse of the exceptional season; but this will scarce suffice. The clemency of nine winters, gave the authorities no right to reckon on perpetual immunity; and the troubles that have crushed them ought to have been foreseen when the first sleeper was laid. So say their accusers, with no mean show of truth.

It was 'shapen in wickedness,' this unlucky line; for its chief promoters were deep in a certain

Crédit Mobilier, which, after a brief, unhealthy blaze, flickered out with an ill-savour of dishonesty. So, as the vast subsidies poured in—forty-five millions from government, besides land grants, and large monies raised on bonds—they flowed through the hands of one Direction into the coffers of the other, in the guise of accommodating contracts. Then, naturally, came the question, how to accomplish the absolutely necessary work at the least cost, preserving a fair outward seeming.*

A rail over the Rocky Mountains.

Hath it not a brave sound, even in these days of engineering Anakim? Bierstadt's famous picture conjures up a chaos of torrents, cliffs, and *cañons;* and we marvel at his hardihood who first brought level to bear thereon. The great painter is doubtless accurate to a leaf and a line; but his brush was wielded in the inner heart of these hills. Travellers through many lands become familiar with disillusions: yet cannot I recal such an imposture as these same Rocky Mountains, approached by railway from the east. From Omaha to Sherman, is all against the collar; but the rise is so gradual, that there seems no change in the dull champaign, adust or

* Vide Appendix A.

hoary according to the season; you are always looking at the same rim of low steep cliffs on the far horizon—at the same muddy creeks, weltering through stunted willows. You mount nine thousand feet above sea-level, without encountering as much broken ground as lies round Aldershot; and the grades, with a very few exceptions, would be child's play to a skilful engineer.

The Directors might have defied King Winter, if, at the beginning, they could have hardened their hearts, like their rivals of the Central Pacific. The cost of forty-three miles of nearly continuous sheds, even with timber felled on the spot, rather dwarfs that of the flimsy plank-fences, hardly stiff enough to stop a clever hunter, let alone snow-waves sweeping over scores of miles. An official, high in authority, averred to us that, for less than half a million of dollars, cuttings might be deepened, embankments raised, and bulwarks fortified, so as to make the line comparatively safe. Therefore, to some extent, out of their own mouths these men are judged.

There has been a change of direction of late; and Vanderbilt is said to control the road. Under the iron sceptre of this truculent old despot, much may perchance be amended. When abuses have come to a certain pass, there is much profit in tyranny.

We reached Cheyenne, 500 miles from Omaha, without grave mishap; and, during the mid-day halt, made our first acquaintance with Western jewellery. Some chains and bracelets, of delicate fragile workmanship, would have seemed more in place at Genoa, or in the old Palais Royal, than here, on the skirts of the wilderness. But, side by side with these, were ponderous gimmals, on which might fitly have been inscribed—

> For the Amal, Amalric's son
> Smid, Troll's son, made me.

The miner, who has made his 'pile,' has grand Gothic tastes, in more ways than one; and likes to see the ruddy metal glitter royally, both on his own person, and on that of his lawful—or lawless—love. Some of the watches, heavily chased in solid gold, would have outweighed any ship's chronometer. But the chief temptation to us Britishers were the moss-agates—quite the loveliest of their kind I have ever seen. The fairy sprays are so perfectly defined, that it is hard to believe real vegetation is not shrined in the crystal. Luckily, the best specimens were unset; so, after much embarrassment of choice, we were able to please our fancies at no ruinous cost.

As we were about to start, a train came in which had been blockaded, for some days, near Sherman. There was scant time to talk: but the Eastward-bound travellers seemed strangely sullen and taciturn. A week later we should not have wondered at such churlishness. There was some sardonic laughter when one of our company asked, in his simplicity —"If there was a chance of our getting right through?"

"You'll hear all about it at Laramie," the other conductor shouted through his grimy, unkempt beard. And so we went each our own way.

That night's halt was at Sherman, the very highest point of the Union Pacific line. Our Professor's barometers, carefully collated, made us 9150 feet above the sea-level. Crossing a deep rugged ravine, early on the morrow, near the Black Hills (the rocks were the very reddest of granite), we got our first and last taste of all the 'savage grandeur' we had looked to find hereabouts. And so, through ever deepening snow-cuttings, we crept on to Laramie—long familiar to us by name.

Six trains lay in port here; and on the morrow

the whole huge caravan set forward—the intelligent Superintendent "hoping that, with luck, we might fetch Ogden within the week." But he looked almost *too* intelligent as he spoke; and there was something ominous in his courteous advice to such as had letters to post, "not to hurry themselves." Moreover, we discovered that the provision-train in attendance carried a full month's provender.

Constantly slackening speed, often stopping, not seldom backing a furlong or so, our carriage sides grating and rasping along the high snow-walls, we made a kind of progress, till, at sundown, some forty miles from Laramie, we came to a full halt.

On the period of rebuke and blasphemy ensuing it is not pleasant to dwell; though it was certainly an 'experience' in its way.

There could be no fear of privation in a Palace Car, chartered and commanded by the Commodore. The prairie-hens, and other delicacies laid in at Chicago, held out bravely; there was wealth of all manner of drink, simple and compounded; and, whether by day or night, our sable servitors were 'all there.' Steady whist, at dollar points, was usually available; varied by occasional plunges in the perilously fascinating

'Poker.' On one occasion, I remember, we sat down—'just to while away an hour before turning in:' we were still 'whiling,' when, almost simultaneously, through the curtained window of our state room peered in the pale winter sun, and the scandalised face of the bride. There was no lack of light literature on board; furthermore, two or three of our company had stories of personal adventure to narrate, with a *real* ring in them, which they told graphically.

Here, I first began to understand the intense bitterness of feud which prevails, and, in spite of preachers and politicians, must prevail along the Indian frontier. The chief spokesman on this subject, though he had, of necessity, been out more than once on the foray, seemed, by nature, little prone to take offence, or think evil of his neighbour: no wild roysterer, or vaunting Drawcansir; but a gentle, domestic being, whose thoughts, even in his schemes of profit, turned oftenest, I am sure, towards the pleasant homestead, just without the hum of San Francisco, where his young wife sat alone. Directly this theme was broached, the man seemed utterly transformed; his quiet face would flush darkly, whilst an evil light came into his eyes, and his discourse—contrary to its usual tenor—was larded with strange oaths.

"There's only one good Indian; and that's a dead one"—was the essence of his simple creed; and I believe it to be shared by many, not really harder of heart than the mass of the humanitarians.

There is not a little of the 'platform' about all this philanthropy, you must remember; and it is tainted occasionally by the spirit of lucre to boot. The chief 'sympathisers' stand, perhaps, above suspicion; but Indian agents, unless they are belied, are less scrupulous than the average of public functionaries; and it may be doubted if the full tale of the subsidies—chiefly of goods—voted annually, ever reaches the Redskin. The fraud, not the good intent, is set down in the account; and 'Spotted Dog,' or 'Flying Cloud,' or whatever other name the chief rejoices in, leaves the Agency with more malice than gratitude at his sullen heart.

To judge the question fairly, you must clear your mind of the Mohican ideal. It would be easier to find Phyllis and Corydon in our Black Country, than Uncas or his sire in Nebraska or Arizona. Possibly, the virtue of stoical endurance does still abide with the dregs of the race; but their brute courage seems a thing of the past: of late years instances can scarce be quoted of Indians confronting armed whites, unless at absurd numerical odds. Does it avail to speak of honour to negociators whose diplomacy is founded on broken treaties; of chivalry to warriors who count babies' curls and girls' tresses among their scalp-locks—the last, perhaps, shorn from heads bowed to the dust with the agony of shame; of mercy or charity to those whose outrages are wreaked on the dead? For mutilation is carried to a science; so that eyes, versed in these ghastly characters, can tell, looking at a corpse, whose hands have been busy in the massacre.

I shall have occasion hereafter to record testimony bearing on the question, whose bias must have inclined rather Indianwards. But it is evident that moral, no less than physical levers, must have a *fulcrum;* and where are you to find one in natures such as these?

In no one point of their home-policy does the American Executive seem to have evinced so much weakness and inconsistency as in their dealings with the Redskin. When the appeals from the frontier can no longer be ignored, or when some deed of unusual atrocity has made even distant ears to tingle, they send out a few squadrons, supported by a regiment of infantry and a battery of light guns, commanded by some Indian-fighter of renown, who has instructions to act 'vigorously.' It may be that the brigadier somewhat exceeds the letter of his orders (for in this infernal warfare the barbarities lie not all on one side); but, at any rate, suppose the savages reduced to that state of salutary awe which is their nearest approach to peaceful citizenship. In nine cases out of ten, before this influence has had time to solidify, appears on the scene a sort of Moderator—usually a civilian,—with powers utterly nullifying those of his military colleague. It is the old story, on a very minute scale: few Republics, founded since the Christian era, have been found liberal enough—unless the crisis be imminent—to allow their generals to act with unfettered hands. Now, the Indian cunning displays itself. In his progress, the Commissioner sees faces innocent of war-paint; if fresh scalp-locks hang in the wigwams, they are not flaunted at the belt of the sententious chief, always ready with his stale, cut-and-dried professions of amity towards the 'Great White Father;' and an odour of peace—not to say of sanctity—pervades the land. When this is reported at Washington, there is triumph amongst the humanitarians; and *largesse* of woollen stuffs and guns cements the treaty, which is to throw all others into the shade. Before the first are worn out, the last-named gifts are in full play. And then the 'fighter' comes to the front again; and the whole dreary farce is repeated, for the fiftieth time.

In a paper, not a fortnight old, I read the account of the massacre of an entire family, in which the grandame, and the baby in the cradle, perished alike; with General Sheridan's remarks thereon.

"When a white man robs," says this plain-spoken commander, "we send him to the penitentiary; when he murders, we hang him. When a Redskin commits both these outrages, we give him more blankets. At this rate, the civilisation of the Indian is likely to progress but slowly."

He writes very much to the point, as it seems to me. On the other hand, if Indian amalgamation be ever so impossible, there is no need to cry for ever, *Delendi sunt.* Drink, disease, and debauchery would play havoc with a nation in its prime—to say nothing of one in the last stages of decrepitude. There is no law more inexorable than that of races: by this law, I believe, these savages are doomed, even as are the Australian aborigines. Human efforts, or errors, may possibly retard, but they will hardly avert the end; and it seems more imminent in the first case than in the last.*

There were presented to us, moreover, other curious lights and shadows of frontier life; for the Commodore had spent much of his youth up in the mining camps, and bore token thereof in the shape of a scar on his broad chest, through which the life had nearly flitted, whilst his antagonist escaped not so easily. And the Senator had practised at the Western bar, in times when matters rolled not smoothly, as now-a-days, in the groove of dull decorous routine; when pleaders did not confine themselves to mere wordy warfare; and when judges were almost forced to follow the example of the famous Lord Norbury, who was ever ready to account for his decisions 'elsewhere,' and carried his pistol-case on circuit as regularly as his wig-box.

Our friend must have had some queer cases to conduct, and some queer clients to boot. Though the sympathies of the country trended chiefly northwards, during the latter part of the Civil War, California and Nevada were turned into a kind of

* Vide Appendix B.

Debateable Land, by the frequent incursions from Texas; so that party-feud was added to other elements of discord. How many and various were these, it is not hard to imagine, when you realise what a strange *congeries* of nationalities were crowded together in a comparatively narrow compass; and remember that each man's hand was not more against the rest of the world than against his brother Ishmaelites, with whom he had, perchance, but one passion in common—the lust of gold. 'Take no thought for the morrow,' was the prevalent motto, of course; and it applied to life no less than to lucre. Listening to these stories of blood and broil, I wondered less at the desperate recklessness of the chief actors therein than at the wild-cat toughness of their vitality: howsoever maimed by shot or steel, the power of rending seemed to abide with them, so long as they could crook a talon or gnash a fang.

The last exploit of one famous Mohock, with whom the Senator had been brought, once or twice, professionally in contact, may be worth recording; it was narrated to the latter by an eye-witness.

Captain Hewson (I am rather vague as to the

heroic name) reckoned, with pardonable pride, over a dozen victims of his knife or pistol—only death wounds counted, remember—and, though scarred like any *vieux de la vieille*, the strength and sleight of his hand rather waxed with years. On this especial night he was not 'on the rampage;' but was consuming a pacific whisky-skin, his feet tilted on the high stove-fender, when there entered the drinking-booth a stranger, likewise of inoffensive demeanour. The new-comer peered round keenly, as though in search of some one; then he walked straight up to the stove, and without uttering a syllable, shot Hewson through the breast as he sate, and, turning, fled away swiftly. The murderer—for this was no homicide even by border-law—had just time to lock himself into an inner chamber, when Hewson hurled at the door, which yielded to the shock; he issued forth again in ten seconds, leaving a corpse behind riddled with five bullets. Steadily and silently—pressing his hand hard on his side—the victor strode back to his seat through the admiring crowd, and replaced his feet on their old resting-place. Then—

"Pull my boots off," quoth he, "and look d—d sharp about it. My old mam" (meaning the mother that bore him) "always said I'd die with 'em on. I don't mean her to crow."

He was dead, almost before his bidding was done; and the autopsy, with which such rare merits were honoured, revealed a wound through the apex of the heart.

Less truculent tales, moreover, beguiled the time. Indeed, Western mining-chronicles would furnish materials for more than one sensational romance; and it would be no romance after all. It is not only below ground that the lodes are 'worked;' or colossal fortunes would not be made and lost within such an incredibly brief space of time. If the stones of California Street—worn down already, though they have been quarried within ten years, by the tramp of eager spectators—could give tongue, they would tell some odd stories of veins mysteriously vanishing, and reappearing just as mysteriously when the shares had ebbed to their lowest, and weak holders were worn out with 'calls.' All's fair in brokerage it appears, and—*occupet extremum scabies.*

But—despite all diversions and distractions, aleatory, literary, or conversational—shall I own how heavily hung the hours? A dead calm at sea is sufficiently trying; but, if you cannot pretend to fish, you make friends with vagrant gulls; and any minute the dark ruffle may line the horizon, bringing the breeze on its back; moreover—bar the Ancient Mariner's luck—the atmosphere carries no intolerable burden, and there is rest for the eye when the sun is low.

But the sameness of these accursed white wastes is never broken by hoof or wing; for the buffaloes have fled southwards long ago, and antelope and elk keep close under the lee of the cliffs, or in the valleys where some acrid herbage under-lies shallower snow; whilst you deprecate the wind as your worst enemy. There is monotony even in the incessant disappointment of moving forward a furlong or so, and then retrograding, as it seems, nearly as far. And the indoor temperature, spite of all precautions, was at times simply stifling; though it was light and pure compared to that of other cars—notably the one alluded to above. That atmosphere, as the Commodore observed, "might have been sliced with a bowie-knife:" it literally haunted me. There was a little excitement, at first, in watching the steam-plough, driven by four strong engines, swish through a drift previously loosened by pick and spade ; but soon it became a question whether the sight was worth the tramp through loose snow, under a blinding glare—we were nearly the hindmost train of the league-long caravan—then it ceased to be a question at all.

Our comrades bore themselves bravely ; and the women, of course, were bravest. But one and all got beat at last. The twitter of our love-birds waxed feeble and faint ; the Professor was as chary of his jests as dead Yorick ; the Commodore's robust appetite could only dally with the savoury meats in which his soul delighted ; the comely face of the Sailor grew lined as with age ; and the Senator, with his solemn straight-cut face, might have sate for a doge in exile. In the last two days of durance, I do not believe that an honest laugh was heard aboard.

On the seventh morning, we had made just six and forty miles ; but cheering news came from the front. Moving stealthily onward, we crossed an eastward-bound train before nightfall, and knew that thenceforth the road was clear. Before dawn we reached Ogden, where the Arlington parted with its fair freight ; and, two hours later, swept along the shore of the Great Salt Lake, glimmering under a level sun.

CHAPTER III.

THE platform was thronged when we rolled into Salt Lake City; and no wonder. During three weeks neither passengers nor mails, to say nothing of merchandise, had come through from the East. And these good people had not only to welcome coming, but to speed parting guests; for the outgoing train carried away the Japanese ambassadors and their suite.

We were not much over-awed by the distinguished foreigners. Under European costume, even solemn Armenians, and stately Turks, can hardly maintain their natural dignity. These puny mortals seemed very husks of men in their ill-fitting garments; and their smooth sullen faces were not improved by their fashionable head-gear, as they flattened their noses—in most cases quite unnecessarily—against the window-panes. Neither did the princesses quite fulfil one's idea of those born in the purple. Certainly, they suffered by contrast with their American *chaperone*—a gorgeous and majestic dame, whose ample charms seemed to dwarf her surroundings, including her own diplomatic spouse.

We had brief time for criticism, however. The Japanese train moved off before we had half got through our introductions, and the inevitable hand-grips ensuing; for the Commodore, the Senator, and the Professor, met divers old acquaintances on the platform. Salt Lake City does not shine in its hotels; and it was decided that the Arlington should continue to provide us with bed and board. So the good car was put into port there and then, and we went forth to lionise.

When the notes of the three aliens were compared, I think the result was disappointment. In summer or autumn, when the frequent fruit-trees are in flower or full bearing, and when the water, that never ceases to ripple through the street-channels, must have a pleasant sound, it is just possible that the town and valley may contain certain attributes of a 'paradise'—using the word in the original Greek meaning. Truly, strangers, not wont to soar into wild flights of enthusiasm, have waxed eloquent over the attractions of the bird's-eye view from the Wahsatch. It is only of late that the place could be reached without long wheel-travel over arid plains and bleak hill-ranges; and much must be conceded to the first impressions of eyes weary of barrenness or sated with monotony. Nevertheless, I think it needs a strong afflatus of the Mormon spirit to gush over the Mormon city.

There is no lack of air, nor of greenery, doubtless, at the fitting seasons. But one hardly looks for close alleys and noisome courts, where building ground may be had for the asking, and where any man who will turn a rivulet may sit under his own vine and fig-tree. I do not cavil at the huge Tabernacle, wherein some twenty thousand can sit at ease; nor at the granite Temple that, ere it is roofed, will swallow up countless dollars; nor at the President's mansion, with its gardens and dependencies; nor even at the pretentious dwellings of certain leading Elders, where bad taste has run riot at no small cost; because these things pertain more or less directly to the hierarchy. Howsoever vain be his creed, no man can be blamed for postponing public convenience to exigencies that he holds divine. But it did occur to us that if some of the large monies, derived from the weekly contributions in kind to the Tithing House, had been thrown into the streets, so as to make the foul quagmire between the *trottoirs* at least fordable in wet weather, it would have been a sage civic policy. And those same streets are sound going, compared to the main highways leading countrywards.

The absence of luxury, under the circumstances, is natural enough, if not laudable; but the absence of ordinary comforts is not so easily accounted for in a city whose inhabitants, financially speaking, must be waxing fat as Jeshurun. The hotels—judging from the complaints of their guests—must be models of mismanagement; and, having proved both, I would back the *cuisine* of most up-country mining camps against the best *restaurant* of Salt Lake; whilst the same characteristics seemed to pervade the entire domestic economy. It may be alleged, of course, that the Saints—never much given to hospitality—are, just now, leading a specially self-contained life; and that the Gentiles sojourning there have rarely, if ever, troubled themselves to mount an establishment—wishing that nought should hinder their flitting so soon as their 'pile' is made. Nevertheless, that so much squalor should co-exist with rapidly swelling wealth and exorbitant prices, is certainly rather a puzzle.

In spite of all the business transacted there, Salt Lake is far from a bustling place. Throughout the forenoon there is a concourse on the pavement of the main Avenue, in the vicinity of the chief banks and telegraph offices; but none of the eager faces, strained voices, or hurrying footsteps that you would notice in Wall or California Street: the nearest bar swallows up each group before it is well formed; and the loungers appear much more intent on cock-tails and apple-jacks than on a serious 'deal.' Yet, every day, there is exchange and barter of interests scarcely less grave than those which are dealt with on the exchanges of New York and San Francisco. What business may be privately transacted in those dingy offices and upper chambers, it would be impossible to guess. A stranger can only record that the city supplies few external evidences of her increasing prosperity.

Brains and capital must find fair scope there in more than one branch of industry; but, if no other commerce thrived, bankers, at least, ought to flourish like bay-trees. Imagine two and three per cent., *monthly*, for monies advanced on securities, real, or nearly as substantial as ordinary mortgages. As an eminent bookmaker observed, after reading a feminine account of a Grand Military, in which long odds were laid on each and every starter—"If *that* ain't good enough, I don't know what is."

Things are widely changed since the primitive days of purism, when blasphemy in public was no venial offence, when strong liquors were only covertly sold, and when the *vierge folle de son corps* dared not show her face ever so discreetly veiled. Tongues wag now with the large Western licence, in the frequent drinking bars, in the vast billiard-saloons, and in the bowling-alleys, where more healthful pastime is found; and in the streets, there is no lack—more's the pity—of bold eyes and brazen brows. But, though the Gentile element is already powerful, it is far from leavening the whole mass; and the Mormon takes both his pleasure and his profit sadly—it may be, more sadly than heretofore.

A sober sedate folk are the males, wearing, for the most part, rather a downcast look; yet, watching their visages narrowly, you will be prone to doubt if humiliation has, in all cases, brought humility, and if forgiveness of enemies be essential to a Saint's salvation. It may have been mere imagination; but

I fancied many countenances bore the reflex of their Chief's expression.

Brigham Young was in custody of the United States marshal at that time, and on his trial for murder in the second degree; but it was by no means a close arrest, and we met him occasionally taking his walks or drives abroad.

A remarkable face, assuredly, and far from attractive; but a certain square firmness of outline saves it from ignoble sensuality; and, though seemingly incapable of benevolence, the deep-set eyes are rather calculating than cruel: nevertheless it is a face that even friends must sometimes have distrusted, and in which foes would hardly look for grace. His photograph does not impress one so forcibly; but, watch the man in the flesh, and in an unstudied *pose*, and see if you can help suspecting that there is solid ground of truth in some of the charges on which he has been arraigned.

Ill deeds, not less than good, thrust each other out of memory; and Western annals teem with such crimes; but the Mountain Meadow massacre is not quite forgotten yet, when saintly hands were dipped wrist-deep in Gentile blood, and knife or tomahawk spared neither woman nor suckling. The outrage was imputed to the Indians, of course, by Mormon advocates; but the balance of proof goes far to show that the few real Redskins engaged in that murderous foray were mere stalking-horses and hirelings. It would be unfair to rely over much on the recent 'Confessions' of one Hickman, who avows himself to have acted, for years past, as bravo, or executioner, to the President and his privy-council; but that obnoxious persons have been, from time to time, quietly suppressed, without scruple as to the means, is beyond doubt; and to many cases, where steel or lead left no traces, the famous Indian verdict would apply—'Died by the visitation of God, under very suspicious circumstances.'

Perhaps, there is nothing in all this to cause much horror or wonderment. Scarcely any faith—false or true—has been founded or promulgated without human sacrifice. The Mormon President might allege that he at least believes implicitly in the Creed which we contemn, and that, in removing its opponents or detractors, he did but smite the heretic after more merciful fashion than did Torquemada or Calvin; if fanaticism can no longer plead exemption from human justice, he has only lived a little too late; and, if private feuds or interests sometimes coincided curiously with religious zeal, I suppose to this, too, he might find historical parallels.

In fine, I am inclined to believe there was sound common-sense in a Gentile's reply to my query, as to "what would ensue if the United States forces were withdrawn from Utah, and the Mormons left once more wholly to their own devices?" He was well posted in the ways of the place and people, my sturdy interlocutor, and could hold his own in a 'free fight' with the best.

"I don't know what *they'd* do," quoth he; "but I know what *I'd* do—make tracks before sundown."

However, if I differ from the sympathisers who found in the settlement by the Salt Lake an Arcadia, replete with pastoral and patriarchal virtues, and void of offence against its neighbour, I cannot withhold a mite of praise, where so much is really due.

There is no mystery—perhaps no great difficulty—in the process which has turned sandy wastes into fertile tracts, sufficing all the colony's requirements, even with the late influx of strangers. The simple word 'irrigation' explains it all. But, if you remember that only within the last quarter of a century have our English farmers developed in earnest the watery wealth of the hill-country, it would be churlish to deny the merit of these ingenious and patient pioneers, who must, for the most part, have worked by the light of nature, with scant theory or practice to aid them; for mechanics and tradesfolk far out-numbered the agriculturists among the early settlers. The rapid increase of the city is not surprising; for in this Western country frame-houses sprung up like mushrooms, and brick-stores like gourds; but the valley, lying betwixt the Great Lake and the lower buttresses of the Wahsatch, ought to keep an abiding place in the chronicles of human industry.

Whilst doing justice to the people, we will not refuse it to the President. Allow that he is stained with all the crimes imputed to him—luxury, avarice, cruelty, and blacker vices yet, if such there be. Still you cannot deny that the man has evinced administrative talent, and tact of no mean order. To have made such materials as he had to deal with not only cohere but work harmoniously, as a rule, implies more than a smattering of political economy. Truly—howsoever unscrupulous may have been their chiefs—the mass of the Mormons have ever been peaceful, not to say feeble folk, and the elements of discord in Salt Lake City in the old times, before the late bitternesses crept in, were probably less than might have been found in any ordinary mining-camp. Nevertheless, in such a mixture of nations and languages there must have been constant conflict of feelings and interests; and Brigham Young contrived—if he did not utilise all these—to keep them at least within decent control. Under his direction, a territory, that thirty years ago was simply valueless, has mounted almost to State dignity; and if, whilst adding to the common wealth, he has filled to overflowing his own coffers, he has but followed the example of certain Viceroys whom we and our forefathers have delighted to honour. How powerful—if not for good—the man has been in his generation, would be proved by one fact alone. Since his health began to fail, politicians have begun to pore more hopefully over the Mormon puzzle; for by his strong influence, and stronger will, all projects of consolidation and mutual conception have hitherto been thwarted, more effectually than by the fears or prejudices of Elders, Council, and people.

It would be hard, at this juncture, to prophesy aright concerning the immediate future of Utah. Retrospective action against polygamy seems utterly impossible; yet scarcely more so, than that it should be connived at hereafter in any American state. Even at Salt Lake it does not seem to have spread of late, if its roots are not loosened in the soil. The fact that a book, like Mrs. Stenhouse's, directly impugning the morality and utility of the institution, from long personal experience thereof, should have been printed and largely sold within the precincts of the city, speaks for itself. How would it have fared with authoress and publisher some five years ago I wonder?

If polygamy be a grave breach of divine as well as human law—the which I am far from denying—the criminals in Utah can plead less excuse of temptation than the average of sinners. Putting such memories in order, I have doubted whether Baltimore, Verona, or Arles—at fair-time—stood highest in the beauty-scale; but, since quitting Salt Lake, I have never hesitated where to assign the palm of homeliness. It is almost incredible, that in a community numbering some 25,000 souls, where—whatsoever may be the inner restrictions of the seraglios—the women-kind walk freely abroad unveiled, a stranger may pass days and weeks without encountering a face or figure worth a second glance, or even a case of ugliness redeemed by graceful gait or eloquent eyes—yet more incredible, that such barrennesss of attraction should exist in Western America.

Rude and plain words; yet, perchance, therefore, the more suited to the subject matter. Certainly, unless he were morbidly uxorious, any man might be satisfied with two or three, at the outside, of such consorts. Of course, if you look on these hard-featured females simply as household drudges, or spinners of webs, there need be no limit to their number, any more than that of slaves on a plantation. But—put them in the lowest scale of help-meets—and you will find much to admire in the courage and obstinacy of the Mormon male.

At first, we are prone to wonder how women are found ready to abdicate all wifely dignity, and feed on mere crumbs of parcelled affection: after a few strolls through Salt Lake City, we cease from thus wondering. The sex, cynics say, is apt to wax exceeding bold when on the verge of perpetual virginity; and a fraction of a spouse—be it ever so 'vulgar'—is, perhaps, preferable to a cipher which cannot be dealt with by any rules of feminine arithmetic. And the goods—if I may speak coarsely—invoiced hither, would have been apt to hang on hand even in that brisk Australian market where, according to the legend, proposals were made through speaking-trumpets, before the good ship 'St. Ursula' cast anchor. *Tout vient à point a lui qui sait attendre*—is an excellent maxim; but, surely, it applies to old maids less than to any other order of created beings; and desperate emergencies need desperate remedies. I am speaking now of the late immigrants and converts: the native damsels are, of course, 'as young as anybody else, if not younger.' But the same stamp of dowdy homeliness seems impressed in all alike; and even for the 'devil's beauty' you may look in vain. At the theatre, for instance, one of the actresses—she was of the blood Presidential, by the same token—had to play a coquette of rather an advanced order; and her costume, though in nowise audacious, was evidently intended to match the part. I have discovered more *chic* in a Quakeress, clad in hodden grey, meditating with folded hands. In fine, I am inclined to believe that considerations of profit or policy, rather than passion, might account for the most of these unholy alliances.

Looking at matters dispassionately, the gulf between the present condition of the Mormon, and complete American civism, does not seem so impassable. There are fanatics, no doubt, amongst the dwellers by the Salt Lake, who would hold out against concession to the last, with the irrational courage of bigotry; but the majority are quite alive to the advantages likely to accrue to Utah so soon as she shall rank as a State. By infinite sweat of brow, and toil of hand, they have made their surroundings pleasant and fertile; nor would they lightly embark on another Exodus, if a vacant Canaan were within ken. The vitality of Mormonism is quite unimpaired; but there are symptoms, everywhere, of the 'old order changing,' and polygamy is already rather a doctrine than a practice. Supposing the rest of their creed be left intact, and they be free to worship after their own fashion, the rising generation may be apt to doubt if the theoretical advantages of this institution are worth isolation from the great Republic and comparative disfranchisement.

Indeed, if the question were, even now, put fairly to the vote of the entire people—Gentiles, of course, being excluded—I believe Conservatism would go to the wall. At any rate, though the Elders may harangue themselves hoarse, it would be a mistake to suppose that the popular feeling on this matter verges on real excitement. Putting aside the covert malice of certain visages (with which, as was afore said, our fancy may have had much to do)—'listlessness' seems best to describe the condition of those who have no immediate voice in the hierarchy or Council, and who are not directly interested in the new commerce which has of late, morally and physically, almost revolutionised Utah.

But this last topic may not be broached at the fag-end of a chapter.

CHAPTER IV.

Mining.

That word strikes the key-note of many thoughts, and hopes, and fears, not in Salt Lake City alone, but for leagues and leagues around it; and even in England it would find sympathetic chords enow. There is the more reason for handling the subject warily; and—under favour—I must needs, here, briefly 'liberate my soul.'

I have never yet puffed any man's wares for hire; in the matters whereof I am about to treat I have no interest, direct or indirect, beyond the sympathy that we must needs feel in the fortunes of friends or acquaintances by whom we have been courteously and kindly entreated; and, up to this moment, I have never been blessed, or cursed, with a share, ever so humble, in any mine, native or foreign. Quasi-anonymous assertions carry but little weight: yet I am fain to hope that my readers will credit me thus far. If it be otherwise, this chapter had best be skipped in its entirety.

After all, singularly little delicacy need be felt in treading on ground furrowed by so many ploughers; or in touching a topic that has been pitch-forked to and fro by savage controversialists, discussed in the leaders of more than one public journal, and ventilated in Congress. Ever since General Schenk set the teeth, not only of his American colleagues, but of divers diplomats, on edge, by appearing on the Direction, the 'Emma Silver Mine' has been so prominently before the public, that others, besides those who have credit and coin actually at stake, may care to hear the truth thereanent. This truth, without colour or ornament, so far as I have been able to trace it, I propose to tell.

Even if force of circumstances had not influenced the choice, I should still have selected this mining ensample; simply because many persons, not at Salt Lake alone, but in California and Nevada, whose interests, as rival owners, were antagonistic to the 'Emma,' concurred in quoting it as the representative of the limestone formation; and, furthermore, because, to the best of my belief, on this spot only have the subterranean resources of Utah been, hitherto, satisfactorily developed and fairly tested.

He must be a very idler, whom mere curiosity would tempt at such a season to traverse some thousand leagues of sea and land; and, besides the Sailor and myself, each and every one of our small company had duties or business far away from Salt Lake. They had been drawn thither by the common object of examining such mines as were attainable, or open to inspection, in the Wahsatch and contiguous ranges, with a special mission to the 'Emma.' Therefore, after brief dalliance in the Mormon Eden, the 'Arlington' rolled forth again, and conveyed us as far as Sandy, some score of miles from the City; where the car was anchored to await our return: the rest of the journey was to be saddle-work.

There was scarce a rent or a stain on the pure white mantle of the Wahsatch, and the air, though not bitterly keen, was pregnant of snow, as we rode over the barren champaign lying betwixt Sandy station and the mouth of Little Cottonwood *cañon.*

Not a tree or a shrub within ken; nothing but the eternal sage-brush, save where a few sour marsh-herbs mark water-tracks soaking sullenly and vaguely through the loam. The soil is, probably, neither better nor worse than that which has been turned to such good purpose along the shores of the Great Lake; and nothing but irrigation, and drainage of the simplest kind, are needed to fit it for culture. There would be fair grazing, if you could put 'heart' into the pasturage; for there is shelter under the lee of the mountains from northerly and easterly blasts; and, even in this exceptionally inclement spring, the frost had gotten no hold of the ground. As it is, the only animal you are likely to encounter hereabouts is the long-eared 'buck-rabbit'—a feeble, foolish creature, with none of the *verve* of the British coney, and an easy prey to man or beast. We saw one coursed down in about three minutes by a mongrel lurcher, scarce out of puppyhood, who, without invitation, had attached himself to our party.

It was winter again, when we were fairly within the jaws of the *cañon;* but, for four miles or so after entering the gorge, we made good progress over a fairly beaten track, and began to think that the good townsfolk had erred in predicting for us 'a rough time.' An artist's eye might find attractions here, even at this dreary season; though the sternness of the huge cliff-walls on either hand is enhanced rather than softened by the fringes of stunted pines, clinging and climbing wherever they can find foot-hold; and there are studies for the geologist, in the rapid and abrupt changes of 'formations' wherever the rocks stand out bare.

A notable feature in the scene are the stupendous granite boulders bestrewing the comparatively level ground near the entry of the *cañon*. There they lie, some singly, some in clusters, as if they had never stirred since they were hurled hither and thither in some pre-Adamite sport or broil. An unscientific mind will almost be tempted to question how, otherwise, they could have come there? For, not only is it impossible to discern the niches above from which they were rent, but usually they differ in grain, texture, and colour from the overhanging cliffs. A whole chapter of glacier-history would be needed to explain the puzzle. At any rate, this freak of Nature has spared the builders of the Mormon Temple infinite time, cost, and toil. By a simple process of drilling, and insertion of wooden wedges, slabs and blocks are detached ready for the mason's hand : neither are there extraordinary difficulties of transport; for such quarries are rarely very accessible. This industry has founded a little hamlet here ; and, should the projected branch-rail from Sandy to the mouth of the *cañon* ever become an accomplished fact, Graniteville will soon find place in the map of Utah.

So we rode on, cheerily enough, incessantly crossing and recrossing, on the rudest of bridges, the stream that struggles down the gorge, till we reached the half-way hut, and halted for a frugal 'nooning.' About a furlong higher, the enemy that had, thus far, only hovered on our flanks, showed himself in force: the snow-wreaths we had passed were light skirmishers; but the drifts ahead marked a battle set in array. It is easy to make metaphors at leisure; but we had neither time nor inclination for such vanities just then; for, as the ground rose more steeply, the fair broad track faded into the narrowest of trails, which it was necessary to follow warily in single file. Here, too, veils and tinted glasses came into requisition; for the glare from the unbroken white surface was intolerable. Glancing aside, I marked a slender iron cylinder peering quaintly over the snow on our right, and questioned my nearest mate—he was a famous native pioneer — as to the use and fashion thereof.

"It's the smoke-stack of an assay-house," he made answer.

And thus I realised, that some four fathoms' depth of the most treacherous of all substances then bore up our horse-hoofs.

If the British shareholder, who is wont to grumble at tardy or intermitted shipments of ore, had ridden in our company that day, I think, being a just man, he would have repented and recanted. To me it seemed simply incredible that the teamsters—despite their reputed recklessness—should venture down with laden sleighs. Yet we met four or five such before we reached Alta City—all mining camps are 'cities' hereabouts. These encounters were not the pleasantest incidents of the journey. Turning aside is a necessity, of course; and so is dismounting, for a riderless horse sinks to the girths the instant he quits the beaten trail. The leading of a floundering *mustang*, through loose snow more than knee-deep, is not quite so easy as it looks on paper; and a stray fore-hoof left its mark on more than one of our party; whilst our poor Commodore, by a sudden plunge of his frightened beast, 'got a nose put on him' that was truly a 'caution' to behold. However the chimneys of Alta City—no walls worth speaking of were visible—received us at last; and, leaving our cattle to be harboured in some sub-nevadean shelter, we crawled up a kind of snow-stair to our own quarters, in the house of the manager of the 'Emma.'

You would hardly expect to light on so cosy a dwelling, near ten thousand feet above tide-level; and there was no lack of homely plenishments: yet, even within doors, there were signs of the season. The paper on the walls was furrowed and wrinkled, like the brow of age, by the terrible pressure on the planks without; and, after this was explained to us, I think some snow-stories, told in Salt Lake City, came home to more memories than mine —specially as the sky, hitherto cloudless, began just then to darken, and the wind to moan. But, if any man had misgivings, he would scarcely have confessed them in presence of the manager. Throughout the wild winter and wilder spring, that sturdy old Rechabite had claven to his post; never asking furlough from his employers, or quarter from the elements. Only the rugged, weather-beaten face was very grave; like that of one who, often confronting danger, has not learned to despise it.

We arrived too late to visit the mine that day, and there were no other attractions out of doors; so, with appetites worthy the occasion, we addressed ourselves to the serious business of the evening meal. They live largely, these stout mountain-folk; and I have fed, in populous cities, on viands infinitely worse cooked than those set bounteously before us. We had brought a jar or so of liquor from the Arlington; for, though our host neither used nor countenanced strong drink, at few seasons or places would a 'hot Scotch' taste more toothsome than early in February, in the heart of the Wahsatch. Then came whist, and pipes innumerable, and then bed—this last quite a triumph of packing: yet I did not hear of much broken rest.

We were afoot early on the morrow; and the first glance at the weather made us bless the luck, or foresight, that had brought us hither in time. It would have been difficult, if not dangerous, to have ridden far in the teeth of the savage *tourmente* sweeping straight down the *cañon*, and progress on foot would have been scarcely possible; for, even where it had not drifted, there was large increase of fresh-fallen snow. From our quarters to the mine's mouth might be some 200 feet of climbing; but wind and limb were sorely tried before we stood, blinded and breathless, under cover in the main driftway.

There is no need of cage or skip here; neither are you entrusted to the uncertain mercies of a man-engine: for a hundred yards or more, after lighting candles in a kind of vestibule, you walk, *à plain pied*, into the heart of the mountain through a tunnel of ample proportions, in which a tramway is laid. Above and below this are horizontal floors, communicating through short vertical or oblique shafts, and numbering, at the time of our visit, seventeen in all. From the centre of each of these floors side-drifts diverge, like the feelers of a cuttle-fish, varying in length from 50 to 300 feet, according to the promise of the ore revealed. The tramway once left behind, progress is no longer luxurious; but, though it is necessary often to stoop, sometimes to crawl, at no one point is there a shadow of real difficulty or danger. Along many of the driftways the daintiest dame might pass dryshod, and with no worse soil of garments than a feather-brush would amend. The veriest ignoramus could not fail to remark the absence of all the drip and slime familiar to subterranean explorers. But this seemed less extraordinary to the Sailor and myself than to Tressilian, —familiar from his childhood with mining ways. Indeed, I fancy the instances are rare where the earth has been penetrated so deeply without the opening up of divers hidden springs. But hitherto the 'Emma' adventurers have encountered nothing worse than surface-water; though this, in inclement seasons, may prove no trivial peril.

Most of our party looked on the surroundings with a professional eye; but the next matter of wonderment to us laymen (once for all, I bracket myself with the Sailor), was the apparent waste of valuable hewn timber. Everywhere—recrossed and doubled at the brink of each shaft, and at the angle of each driftway—we saw a network of stout joists and square beams, till it seemed as if half a forest must have been swallowed up here. Indeed our conceptions did not much outrun the truth; and it is fortunate that the wooden wealth of these hills will be, for years to come, practically inexhaustible: though there are grievous gaps in their ranks, they still hold their own gallantly—'the shadowy armies of the pine.'

But there is really no waste of labour or material here. The 'caving' of the soil or rock is the very bane of western miners; and by no care or cost can absolute insurance be effected against this disaster, as has been proved over and over again at the famous 'Comstock Lode' in Nevada, where the quartz, from the toughness of its texture, must be far less prone to collapse than the Wahsatch limestone.*

The temperature of the workings was singularly level: the intense outer cold scarcely penetrated beyond the vestibule; and, if the atmosphere in some of the extreme driftways was somewhat dense and heavy, it was never absolutely oppressive; neither did the lowermost shaft exhale the hot mephitic fumes that meet you before you have descended far into most metalliferous mines.

It was rather weary work, the incessant clambering of ladders, and dodging of beams, and creeping in single file through passages where one could rarely stand erect. But, even to us *flâneurs*, each step brought something of interest.

* Vide Appendix C.

Of course, the quality can only be determined by assay; though skilled miners are often surprisingly accurate in their guess-work. But, when a simple code of signs and tokens is once mastered, it does not need an expert's eye to trace ore through a limestone formation. Almost all the workings, examined on that and the ensuing day, were fresh since October last; and quite independent of that vast treasure-chamber which first made the mine famous, and which its opponents characterise as an exhausted 'shell.' They diverged, as was aforesaid, infinitely; but each one that my companions tested—and that the work was not done negligently I can aver—proved more or less remunerative. The veins would vary from a mere thread, to a belt broadening beyond the furthermost pick-mark; but there was always presence of ore; and always, brightly or faintly, the baser soil was tinted with those tender shades of colour that are only laid on by the pencil of the Gnome.

I say 'soil,' advisedly; for you can scarcely dignify as 'rock' matter so friable. A common hunting knife makes deep impression; and six or seven tons daily might easily be dislodged by a practised miner. Proving this, one ceases to wonder at the paucity of hands employed here—not two score, including every official.

It is hard for an unscientific pen to set forth these points lucidly; but ocular demonstration makes it easy to understand how, by simple cubic measure and comparison of weight, the amount of ore included in this net-work of lateral drifts and vertical shafts can be accurately calculated. Moreover, in this 'prospecting,' the quality of the ore can be estimated with no less certainty than the quantity, if it be sampled without fear or favour, and honestly assayed.

The importance of this last condition is obvious; for, however just in the letter, it would hardly be just in the spirit, to bring up the balance by the addition of rare isolated specimens, such as may be found in almost any mine, whose proper place is on the shelves of a cabinet. On the present occasion two or three such—one assaying near 1300 dollars—were purposely set aside.

Though the value of the ore thus 'exposed' can be so nicely calculated, certainty, or even absolute confidence, with the most experienced miner ceases here; for the caprices of the veins, to say nothing of the 'pockets,' as the large isolated deposits are termed, are infinite. As a rule, however, the coy metal seems to wax kinder from pursuit; and the richest ores are oftenest struck in the deepest workings.

The rage of the *tourmente* was abating when we saw light again, though heavy flakes still cumbered the air. But, if the day had not been so far spent, outdoor work would have been impracticable; for the fresh snow would not carry, and the drift against the front of our 'stoop,' yesterday scarce two cubits deep, was heaped up now in a wall shoulder-high. Communication even with the City below was not so easy; and, I believe, our sole visitor that afternoon was a rotund, ruddy urchin, bearing a message from a telegraph office.

He was very self-possessed, this small envoy; and a *largesse*, that must have transcended his wildest hopes, in no wise altered his calm stolidity. Questioned as to how he had clomb up hither, he 'reckoned, he'd squirmed along somehow.' Indeed, to us watching his downward progress, he seemed to make no more impression on the feathery drifts than might have been left by a weasel or a bull-frog.

And we, on our parts, got through the evening

'somehow.' But, though there were no blue devils in our company, the rarefied atmosphere had begun to tell more or less on all who had not been previously acclimatised. The Sailor suffered terribly from headache; and, for myself, I began to understand what James of Scotland must have endured, when

> At each turn he felt
> The pressure of the iron belt;

for I had brought a severe chest-cold out of the blockade. I did not know till afterwards—or I might, perchance, not have taken things so easily—that lung-inflammation is the very pest and bane of the mountain miners. Oddly enough, it seems more fatal to strong men than to women and weaklings.

The next morning broke clear and cloudless, and, rising betimes, we completed before noon the exploration of the 'Emma;' so that Tressilian was enabled to visit two other mines, or rather shafts, sunk hard by. The most distant of these might have been a long rifle-shot from our quarters; but every fathom of steep ascent through deep, loose snow, tells heavily, as all mountaineers will aver; and our stalwart comrade had had rather more than enough of it when he returned about sundown, especially as he had seen nothing to repay his toil. The reason of this will be made plain hereafter.

Though the time had passed neither unprofitably nor altogether unpleasantly, I think we were all glad to get the 'route' on the morrow. Whilst our companions tarried to inspect yet another mine, the Sailor and myself went down to Alta City. We were surprised to find it such good going; but the snow at these heights hardens rapidly, and sleigh traffic below had already begun. Under ordinary circumstances nothing would be found in Alta more notable than in other hill camps; but it presented, now, a very curious spectacle. Till I stood in, or rather on, the street of that hamlet I never appreciated the potency of drifting snow brought to bear on human handiwork.

I saw something like it, years ago—chamois-hunting in the Savoy Alps—when the autumn fall had begun, and we were glad enough to find a night's shelter in the uppermost *châlet* of the *Allée Blanche*, deserted long since by the cowherds. But there, the uncouth hovel seemed to match not ill with the desolation around; no sign of animal life was within ken; and only by our own voices, or the whistle of a marmot, was the dead silence broken. Here, there were tokens not of life alone, but busy life, and certainly no lack of sounds. Yet Pompeii was scarce more completely, if more durably, entombed than Alta. Over the humbler habitations the snow swelled half way up the chimney-stack; small shafts were pierced to admit light and air, otherwise the population lived like prairie-dogs. Into the principal store, a fair two-storied frame-house in its normal condition, we descended through a cutting abutting on a gable window, and down a ladder fixed within. But, if these stout mountain folk had been bred and born within the Arctic circle, they could not have taken things more coolly. Round the stove of the store in question, there was the usual smoking, chewing, argumentative crowd; the trade over the counter seemed unusually brisk; and, with large experience of Western hospitality, I cannot call to mind having been, within the same space of time, so often solicited to 'smile.'

We all made tracks for the plain about noon; my comrades mounted as before, whilst I embarked in a sleigh also bound down the *cañon.* I would not wish to sit behind a more skilful or intrepid whip than my Judicial charioteer: but, more than once, I wished myself back in the saddle; for so much extra exercise was not good for such a cough as was racking me. The track was intersected by multitudinous dips and hollows, some mere gutters, some almost 'gulches' in breadth and depth. In these last we would come to a full stop; and only emerged by dint of much snorting, rearing, and plunging, with a shock like to dislocate the back of the sleigh; albeit it was expressly built for rough usage. However, at the half-way hut we left broken ground behind; and glided on at top speed over a fairly level track—the snow waxing shallower and less reliable, till it softened into slush at Graniteville. Thenceforward, we were fain to trust to wheels.

Such wheels as they were! The Judge's buggy had, by mistake, been sent back to Salt Lake, and the only spring vehicle which Graniteville could boast was hopelessly out of gear; so we chartered a goods-dray to convey us across the plain. It was a change of motion, no doubt; very much like the change from pitching to rolling in a heavy cross sea. At first we made little headway; for the driver, a swarthy beetle-browed half-breed, would only plod along at a foot's pace—rather, I fancied, with intent to vex his passengers, than out of mercy to his beasts. The twilight deepened and darkened; and still the twinkling lights that showed where the Arlington lay anchored at Sandy seemed no nearer. At last, waxing desperate with aches and weariness, I proposed a drink all round, with a special invitation to our driver. Now, my hunting-bottle, holding nearly a pint, was filled, not with mild 'old rye,' but with whiskey from the Alta store, which, if less potent than that famous liquor which slew men at rifle range, carried abundance of fire and sting. The merest sip sufficed the Judge and myself; but the half-breed drained the flask. The draught acted like a witch's potion. The dull black eyes began to roll and lighten, the slouching shoulders were straightened, the flaccid hands gripped the reins savagely; and, whirling the long lash round his head, he crowded up his team with a will. It was a weird, fantastic journey, the rest of it, like the hurry-skurry of a nightmare; weltering through sloughs and mud-holes, splashing through marshy pools, jolting over half-buried logs or boulders, and taking a rivulet or so, as it seemed, in our stride; with a running accompaniment of yells and thong-cracking. Remonstrance would have been absurd; we could only press our feet against the rail of the dray, and 'let her rip.' Nevertheless, there was method in the half-breed's madness. If he did not always keep the road, he kept his line; and drunkard's luck brought us to Sandy at last—more thoroughly bemired, than if we had been riding to hounds over Naseby Field after heavy rains.

The good old car looked cozier than ever, with its lights, and curtains, and garnished tables; the cheerful countenances of our coloured brethren had gotten an extra polish; and Krug's 'dry creaming' seemed improved in flavour. But we all turned in betimes; and, before we were well awake, on the morrow, were rolling back to Salt Lake City.

CHAPTER V.

My personal researches into the mineralogy of Utah, I am sorry to confess, began and ended in Little Cottonwood *cañon;* for when the rest of the party, after two days' respite, went off prospecting again, the doctors expressly forbade my venturing again into the high snows. So I remained behind to be physicked and blistered at their pleasure; the Sailor, in the kindness of his heart, electing to keep me company.

It may seem presumptuous, to speak at all concerning matters in which one has such scant experience; but Tressilian did not waste his abundant opportunities; and on his observations I can rely, as implicitly as if the facts had come within mine own ken. Furthermore, where there is such conflict of interests, an unbiassed opinion may, perchance, be worth recording.

Though individual reports may, for obvious

reasons, have outrun the truth—so far as the truth has been ascertained—I do not, in my conscience, believe that we in England have formed an exaggerated estimate of the mineral wealth of Utah. That idea of the superior certainty of the 'fissure-veins' running through quartz, will, probably, soon be ranked among buried fallacies. The fluctuations of the Stock Market at San Francisco are unexampled elsewhere; and almost all the mines, there dealt with, lie in the granite formation. The 'fissures' have an awkward habit of losing themselves in the innermost bowels of the earth, and it may need infinite toil and cost to knit the broken clue; sometimes it is never recovered, or, worse still, picked up at hazard by some neighbouring explorer.

The silver ores of the limestone formation appear usually, it would seem, in a network of veins, swelling out at intervals into arteries or 'pockets;' and the danger, of course, is that, the artery once exhausted, the precious current may cease thenceforward to flow. But it may be long before the heart of the mountain be drained; and, in any case, I fail to see how a lesser risk attends mining in granite. As for permanence of profit, a property, paying dividends through a couple of centuries or so, may be considered fairly durable. Now, some Chilian mines, almost identical in formation with those of the Wahsatch, with the rudest appliances, have outlasted this date without sign of exhaustion; and Germany, I believe, can supply still more forcible parallels.

Furthermore, it must be remembered that the cost of working quartz and limestone cannot even be compared. In the one case, you have to deal with a substance so hard and tenacious as sometimes only to be conquered by dint of drill—in the other, with matter so friable that the pick must often be plied warily lest the treasure-seeker fare like Tarpeia.

Yet I am far from inferring that capital should be sown broadcast in the Utah *cañons*; or that even the modest aspiration of 'small profits and quick returns' can always be realised here. It is undoubtedly true that, with one or two exceptions, the mineral resources of the country have only been prospected by a few surface workings and shafts driven almost at random. This state of things cannot possibly endure; but, whilst it does endure, the fact cuts both ways.

Very few Utah mines, hitherto offered to the public, have been so far opened up as to enable even an expert to speak confidently as to their probable value. It is probable, of course, that some of these will eventually prove more remunerative than the 'Emma.' Only the *development* of this mine, thus far quite unparalleled in the district, warrants the details given above. At any rate, had it been otherwise, I should have sought elsewhere for an example; or, failing this, have ignored the subject altogether. A tinge of the gambling spirit must ever attend the search after the 'irritaments of ills:' but prudent adventurers will prefer a modest certainty to superb probabilities; and it is next to impossible to guess, even approximately, at the value of a property prospected only by a single shaft, and one or two cross-drifts or 'winzes.' For this reason, that afternoon's toil through the Wahsatch snows was to Tressilian labour in vain; and to this is to be attributed the fruitlessness of most of his later explorations.

Another point should never be lost sight of. Whilst things remain in their present condition, the quantity of ore must be of subordinate importance to its quality. Even in the case of the 'Emma,' where, in ordinary seasons, no great difficulties of transport exist, the freightage per ton amounts to thirteen pounds sterling when it touches English ground; and mines more remote or inaccessible must, clearly, pay heavier toll. Second-class stuff, which, in time to come, may bear no mean value, is now not worth loading on the drays; and large masses of ore, actually exposed, may be practically useless as treasure-trove on a desert isle.

The one great *desideratum* of this country is smelting power. Efforts have already been made in this direction; but they are the merest tentatives; and it were easier 'to drink up Esil' than to tackle the mineral resources of Utah with the toy-appliances hitherto brought to bear thereon. Doing ample justice to American skill and energy—I question whether this grave problem can be worked out, without help from our side of the Atlantic. I hear from reliable sources that there are smelting secrets, and, as it were, sleights of hand, which can scarce be imparted by an instructor ever so willing to pupils ever so diligent. If a man be not to the manner born, such can only be mastered by long study and practice at the head-quarters of the trade; and this applies not only to the officials, but, in some sense, to the working rank-and-file. It would need, perhaps, the importation of an entire 'plant' to make a concern, adequate to the exigencies, work smoothly and profitably; but, speaking under correction, I can see no insuperable difficulties here. In almost every Western mining camp, of any importance, Wales and Cornwall are fairly represented; and the men, who now cross the Atlantic by twos and threes, could surely be tempted to emigrate in a body, especially when the expatriation need only be for a term; for this class are, as a rule, wise enough to prefer large fixed emolument to any precarious chances. About the emolument there can be no question. When a working miner, capable of nought beyond plying pick and spade sturdily, can earn from three to five dollars daily, being liberally boarded to boot, it is easy to calculate what manner of hire really skilled labour might command.

Neither should I apprehend any grave obstacles or dangers from native prejudice or jealousy. With all their national vanity, and desire to keep American market and produce entirely under American control, the folks out here easily recognise where they must perforce rely on foreign aid; and, so long as the necessity existed—as it must exist for years to come—they would be no more likely to annoy the useful aliens, than to turn away a customer because he worshipped Brahma.

The present high price of coke is, no doubt, a serious drawback; but the rates were lowered even during our brief stay; and, if there be any leaven of truth in the reports of recently discovered coal-fields, the supply may soon nearly equalise the demand, and Utah will not need to envy Pennsylvania her 'diamonds.'

For the sake of a country where we received no small kindness, and wherein many Old World interests are already bound up, I have good hope that, before we are much older, a stout tree transplanted —root, bole, and branch—from the black Cambrian forest, may flourish under the lee of the Wahsatch hills. British capital has been risked lavishly, often enough of late, on wilder ventures, with less tempting prospect of prompt and large return.

Albeit in poor visiting form, I contrived to struggle through the mud, in some places axle-deep, up to Camp Douglas, to return the call of General

Morrow; and I had reason to rejoice at having made that effort.

The officers of the American standing army, as at present constituted, need not fear comparison with those of any regular service with which I am acquainted. They are great readers, as a rule, and extend their studies beyond purely professional subjects; but you will find little of Prussian pedantry here; and West Point, with perhaps less congenial material to work upon, turns out as sterling stuff as issued from Saumur or Sandhurst in their palmy days. They contrast still more favourably with the crop of ready-made soldiers that sprang up, so rankly, during the Civil War.

Do we not remember—some of us with good cause—those bragging brigadiers, cursing colonels, and crapulous centurions, who, when they could not bully, were forced to cajole their men, to keep up any show of discipline, and whose uniform always seemed a masquerade or disguise? These worthy creatures were, doubtless, well adapted to the professions for which they were originally intended; but they never could realise that something beyond courage and patriotism is needful to make a perfect soldier. They could fight, certainly, after a fashion;

and they could talk like stump-orators about American grandeur and British perfidy; but the drilling of a squad, or the giving a decent word of command, was not in their province; and tactics were to the majority what Pure Mathematics are to the vulgar.

Things are wonderfully changed now. The U. S. A. officers seem no more inclined to slur over their duty than their European compeers; their training embraces the theory as well as the practice of their profession; and, if their appointments would not always pass muster at our dress-parades, slovenliness and squalor have quite disappeared.

If Anglophobia still prevails to any extent, where political leaven is not at work (the which I take leave to doubt), no class is so free from its influence as the higher grades of this service. During our Western tour, we heard many subjects freely discussed in military circles—including the Alabama question, then at its knottiest point: but we did not meet with a single exception to the general kindliness of feeling towards the mother country; and I am sure this went far deeper than mere surface-courtesy.

General Morrow had had large experience of

frontier life, and his quarters were a perfect museum of Indian curiosities; though there were more trophies here of peace than of war. Indeed, though he spared not the sword on occasion, he was famous for his tact in dealing with the savages; and amongst the buffalo robes, and bear-claw necklets, were tokens of amity from more than one formidable Sachem. Therefore I was curious to learn, whether he could dispute or modify the character I had heard assigned to these tribes. He only shook his head rather sadly, and confessed, with evident reluctance, "that you could trust the best of them just as far as you could see him; not a gunshot further." I gave up the Redskin after this, I own; for it was impossible to look in the speaker's face and doubt the charity or honesty of his verdict.

The small-arm system of the American army is in process of remodelling, and several rifles were then on trial at Camp Douglas. Two or three of these made excellent practice up to 600 yards range—the longest at which we saw them tested. A modification of the Martini-Henry, from the famous Hartford factory, scored, I think, the most points for accuracy and rapid loading; but, though somewhat lighter and better poised than the English pattern, the cartridge-cases seemed apt to hang, after incessant firing, from the heating of the chamber. A repeating carbine on the Winchester principle, not a very recent invention, impressed us most favourably: easily manageable from horseback; with very slight recoil, considering its penetration and straight trajectory—not liable to get out of order with common care—it appeared the perfection of a weapon for desultory or frontier warfare.

We were twice or thrice at the camp after this visit; and, on one occasion, witnessed a review of the small garrison. The dressing of the line was very creditable, though not much attention seemed paid to the 'sizing' of companies; and the marching in quick time was fairly steady, with a springiness that looked very like work. So much for the infantry. However efficient on scout duty or in border-fighting, the American trooper must always make a sorry show on parade. 'Setting up' can scarcely be included in the drill; if the trapping and accoutrements were better cleaned, the hideous spatter-dashes over the stirrups would be fatal to smartness; and both men and horses seem singularly independent of the riding-school.

Though we had made some cheery acquaintances

at Salt Lake—notably 'Dick' of facete memory, and that convivial Captain, who, 'just to prove that he bore no malice,' was always ready to 'smile'—I cannot remember to have been so bored in any town, unless it was at Geneva in early spring. Therefore, very meekly, I accepted the necessity, according to the doctors, of seeking a more genial climate without delay. Indeed, the Mormon City, lying 5000 feet above sea-level, at this season of melting snow is not the likeliest place to cure obstinate pneumonia. We were loth—the Sailor and I—to leave the old Arlington, and our comrades, in the lurch; but the contingency had been foreseen before their departure, and they had, moreover, strongly advised our moving westwards without awaiting their return. So the last afternoon of February found us twain fairly embarked on the Central Pacific, and rolling across the dreary desert dividing Ogden from the Humboldt hills.

A singularly monotonous journey, for the first twenty-four hours at least. Always the grey sage brush, streaked with ghastly white patches here and there, where the alkali crops up through the acrid soil; lines of stunted alders and willows showing where the Humboldt river, or a tributary turbid as itself, welters sullenly along—a country that could never have had natives, and where the few settlers along the rail look like exiles—a country that tempts the traveller to take his uttermost pennyworth out of the sleeping-cars.

Halting for breakfast at Elko, we made acquaintance—at prudent distance—with the Indian, in flesh and blood. Till now, I had thought that about the lowest grade of clothed humanity was to be found in the Upper Valais. I altered my opinion that forenoon. Truly, here there was no special physical deformity; but the moral *crétinism*, so far as could be judged by outward signs, was even more remarkable.

Could those blear-eyed beldams, crooning a low discordant plaint, and stretching forth skinny claws for alms, be the sisters of 'Little Fawn' or 'Laughing Water'? Could that draggled, bloated creature, suckling a *papoose* wrinkled and wizened like a changeling, ever have given birth to braves? Could those shambling, knock-kneed loungers, sodden with the fire-water for which they still craved, ever have backed a wild *mustang*, or met a foe fairly with bow and spear?

It would be manifestly unjust to take these outcasts, whom their own tribe might have disowned, as types of the Sioux or Apaches, even in their present condition; and mendicants, of whatsoever nation or language, only differ by degrees of abasement. Nevertheless, the spectacle was exceedingly suggestive; and, before we left Elko, my last spark of Redskin romance was quenched for ever and aye.

So we travelled on without an incident worth recording; neither was there any notable character on board our sleeping-car, unless it was a certain Virginian, who might, possibly, have been useful to a Temperance lecturer.

This eminent person—he represented himself as a kind of deposed prince in his own country—was decidedly the worse for liquor when we first saw him at Ogden; and he was none the better for it, when, with much difficulty, we evaded him on the Oakland steam-ferry. The phases of his prolonged drink were curious, chiefly from their inconsistency. Having previously averred that his funds were at the lowest ebb, and that he had scant hope of replenishing them, he would provoke us to 'euchre' for fabulous stakes; and, when the challenge was declined—not always, I fear, quite courteously, for he became a nuisance at last—he would descant, with infinite gravity, on the evils of gambling, which, combined with Northern oppression, had brought ruin on his house. Next, having been assured that we had no intention of crossing the Potomac, he would proffer commendatory letters to some shadowy kinsman, still all-powerful in the Dominion; though what office, or what relationship towards our drunkard, he bore, was never clearly defined: 'ex-ticket-collector, and stepfather twice removed'—was my comrade's idea of it. Lastly, he would wax maudlin over the wrongs of the South, and vengeful over the prospect of retribution; but, when the tremulous lips began to stutter about 'chivalry,' it became too shameful for ridicule. We rejoiced when stertorous sleep rid us of his company.

Had we still been on the Union Pacific, we should have been seriously disquieted ere this as to obstacles ahead; for, by sundown, we were within the roots of the Sierra, and on steady ascent, once more through deepening snow. But the stout sheds held their own bravely; and through some two score miles of these we passed without let or hindrance;

till, soon after midnight, Summit Station was attained: then, with always increasing speed, we bore down towards the Pacific.

The morning broke loweringly; but, luckily, the mist lifted just before Cape Horn loomed in sight. Round this huge promontory the rail winds at an angle, wonderful even on this line of zigzags and curves. There is not a pretence of fence or parapet to prevent you from looking sheer down into a gorge over two thousand feet deep; at the bottom of which winds a dusky yellow thread, that to one standing on its banks, would seem a broad yeasty torrent. The Nevadas are as rife, as the Rocky Mountains are barren, of the picturesque; but we met, elsewhere, no 'effect' to compare with this.

By this time, the sheds were left behind; the cuttings were rarer and shallower; the overladen pines, on either hand, had half shaken off their burden; whilst holm-oaks, mountain ashes, and other hardy trees, had begun to appear; and we felt that we were really escaping from the enemy who so long had 'held us with his glittering eye,' when not actually in his clutches. With each mile of descent the air and the scenery waxed softer; till on a southerly slope, under the lee of a belt of woodland, we came upon a real meadow of untainted green. Then quoth the Sailor—we were standing together on the outer platform of the car—

"Thank God! We're clear of the snow at last." To the which devout exclamation his mate said 'Amen,' heartily.

In very truth, during the last month I, for my own part, had been working steadily round to the Scandinavian notions of Hela. On the farthest verge of a distant landscape, or cunningly disguised in a *granita*, snow may possibly be unobjectionable. But in any other shape or form whatsoever—in drift or field, solid or liquescent, falling or fallen, blinding-bright in sun or opaque in shadow—it is to me, henceforward, an abomination only to be confronted on urgent need. If in search of rest or recreation, rather than to Chamounix or Zermatt, I would betake myself to the Essex marshes, yea, or to Mewstone-by-the-Sea.

Even the descent from one of the higher Alpine passes into the Lombard plain, would give you but a faint idea of this sudden plunge from the rigour of winter into the maturity of spring. Under the spurs of the hills nestled trim homesteads, half buried in orchards, under whose eaves the vines were already in tendril; everywhere the tender meadow-grasses were flecked with flowers; and, before we had advanced far into the valley, wheat was stirring in green waves under the westland breeze.

The rainy season was barely ended; for the Sacramento river was still in flood, and in possession of some of the low-lying suburbs. It seemed a busy thriving city, so far as one could judge from the throng and turmoil around the station, which is not in the heart of the town. Indeed, Sacramento is nominally the State capital, and the seat of local government; albeit its importance, social, political, and commercial, is trifling, compared to that of San Francisco. Thenceforward, the journey, to an ordinary traveller, becomes again monotonous; though an agriculturist might look eagerly and enviously at the rich alluvial country stretching away on either side of the rail. Knowing that the land, though seldom or never manured, is cultivated with all modern mechanical appliances, you are puzzled, at first, to account for the sparseness and insignificance of the farm-buildings. Around the homestead itself there may be a few huts and outhouses ; and, here and there, on the edge of a tilth, or at the corner of a grazing-ground, are rude lodges for the shelter of horses or cattle ; but there are few, if any, of the barns or garners that you would expect to find on these vast corn lands. The peculiarity of the climate easily accounts for this. After the rains have once ceased, for months to come, the earth is not moistened even by dew. So the ripe brown swathes, often not bound into sheaves, lie as they fall, till they are threshed, winnowed, and sacked in open air, like the crop of Araunah.

Night had fallen, long before we reached Oakland ; and we were forced to grope our way on board the steam-ferry through a storm of wind and rain. The gusts swirled savagely, even up the land-locked bay ; but the square solid craft made small account of the puny billows ; and, soon, we found ourselves at the very uttermost point of our long journey,

Down by the beautiful Balboa Seas.

CHAPTER VI.

THE 'Grand Hotel' where we were lodged, may be taken as a fair ensample of its own class. With less of garish display, there is infinitely more luxury here than can be found in the most pretentious New York *caravanserai.* To begin with, you are not infested by an incessant sirocco from over-heated flues; the arrangement of apartments is nearly perfect; the table is as good as any other managed on the wholesale American system; and, finally, if you dispense with a sitting-room, the day's entire expense is covered by three gold dollars —little more than half the Eastern tariff.

We bore credentials to a chief authority at the 'Grand.' Lacking these, we might not have lighted on such good quarters; for the house was full nearly to the roof-tree—many bachelors and small families being permanent boarders. In point of comfort my own apartment left nothing to be desired. The oriel window of the sunny *salon* looked across a small *place*, down Montgomery Street, the gayest thoroughfare in the city. In the rear were bed and bath room, *en suite*; spacious enough for any taste, and magnificent to one who, for a month past, had been dressing, so to speak, by inches. These details are set down in the very faint hope that some large-minded London host, in making future 'improvements,' will condescend to take a hint from the farthest West. The like accommodation—barring the genial outlook—can, doubtless, be furnished, in our own metropolis to those who count not the cost; but, till they are brought within the compass of travellers of modest means, a blot will abide on our hotel economy.

We had our last taste of foul weather on board the Oakland ferry; and, thenceforward, the climate amply fulfilled its warranty. Indeed, the next day's sunshine was so tempting, that my mate and I concluded to defer the presentation of our letters, and the exploration of the city, till the morrow; and drove out incontinently to the Cliff House—the favourite afternoon resort of all San Franciscan idlers.

This is a long low frame-house, perched, as its name implies, on the very verge of the Pacific ; the balcony literally overhangs the ocean, and, when the sea is wild, is drenched by the spray. As you sit here, right over against you, distant a cable's length or so, rise the famous Seal Rocks, the basking-place and play-ground of the great sea-lions. There is scarce a day when they may not be counted by scores ; some lying, like big brown logs, in heavy slumber ; others weltering clumsily to and fro over the slippery shelves, or diving deftly into a rising surge ; and, ever and anon, the echoes of the cliffs are waked by uncouth sounds, betwixt roar and bellow, the tokens of their sport or anger. They seem peaceable folk enough, as a rule ; albeit some, of vaster bulk or fiercer temper, arrogate to themselves special nooks, and resent trespass savagely. One huge brute, the tyrant of his tribe—his weight was set at over 1500 lbs.—kept ever solitary state on a certain pinnacle ; and the very lifting of his grim grey head scared intruders. In honour of him who did his spiriting so gently at New Orleans, this Sachem was christened General Butler.

But not only the gambols of the *Protei pecus*

tempted us to linger there so long. After being nipped by raw mountain winds, weighed down by leaden skies, or half blinded by snow-glare, it was like a draught of fresh life to rest in the quiet sunshine, fanned by a breeze coming straight from Hawaii, and watch the sparkle and ripple of the tide rising lazily; for there is scarce a fathom's difference betwixt the height of ebb and flow. Setting aside one or two accessories, it was an ordinary sea-side scene after all; but I have looked on miracles of nature with gratification less keen. Even so said my comrade; and the day was waning when we turned city-wards again.

Despite our pleasant first impressions, I should counsel a stranger to approach the Pacific otherwise. The Cliff House road in itself, though much frequented, is by no means attractive. There are divers issues from the city; but every one of these is rough travelling, and more or less hampered by tramways; the sight of cemeteries on either hand, even if you escape a whiff of incremation from the Chinese burying-ground, is not exhilarating; and, though you get used to the throng of vehicles after a while, the whole thing savours too much of a suburban 'outing.' A far better plan is to drive southwards out of the city, past the quaint old Mission, and follow a road, steep but admirably graded, to the top of the seaward hills. Looking back from the summit, you have a more perfect panorama of the town, and San Josè Bay, than can be gained from any other point with which I am acquainted. After a mile or so of rather abrupt descent, you come on the fairest piece of trotting-ground within leagues of San Francisco; and, if your cattle are fast enough, they can 'hold a 3.20 gait,' till, sweeping round some barren *dunes*, you break straight out upon the sands—at most times of tide so firm and level, that there is no need to draw rein till your wheels spin through the feathery foam.

The next forenoon was taken up in delivering credentials: it is almost needless to say that one or more of these bore the address of the Bank of California. Waiting a few seconds till the manager was at leisure, we watched the cashiers at their busy work. After familiarity with the frayed, greasy, greenbacks, it was refreshing to see cheques exchanged for piles of noble twenty-dollar pieces, or, more rarely, for 'gold-notes,'—crisp and ruddy, as though stained with the essence of the royal metal. For California has a mint and standard of her own, and will have naught to do with Eastern currency: greenbacks, at the usual discount, are a legal tender; but, to proffer them in discharge of a debt of honour, would be a solecism past forgiveness.

None, who have come hither under like circumstances, will doubt the nature of our reception in the manager's room. We were not less kindly and courteously entreated elsewhere; and, before night, we had been made free of both the 'Union' and the 'Pacific.' The former is, I believe, the most frequented by foreigners; but I always infinitely preferred the latter club, though it had no coffee-room privileges, chiefly because there one heard and saw so much more of real Franciscan life.

A large, lusty, liberal life it is; though the pace, a little forced sometimes, must needs tell heavily on fragile constitutions or delicate nerves. After brief experience thereof, you begin to understand a certain peculiarity attaching to this city. With ordinary precautions against chills, the climate is exceptionally healthy, and the table of longevity maintains a fair average; but cases of sudden death are common, and lingering maladies comparatively rare. The silver cord, here, seems more prone to snap than to fray.

The 'free lunches' are a *spécialité* of the place. In the bar-rooms of all the principal hotels, and scores of others besides—to say nothing of the clubs above mentioned—from noon till about two o'clock, a table is spread with soups, stews, hot and cold meats, and multifarious relishes. All who choose may enter, and eat their fill, gratuitously, on the understanding, but not on the express condition, that they shall consume a quarter-dollar's worth of liquor. Rather an unprofitable speculation at first sight; but the originators thereof probably argued that a man could feed but once in a forenoon, whereas he might drink illimitably; and, like most calculations founded on human frailty, their estimate has proved correct.

The Franciscan of the upper class, banker, broker, lawyer, or merchant, lives rather in the continental fashion; indeed, the French element is strong here. Rising early, after a hurried breakfast he betakes himself to his office; and, there, or on the Change in California Street, toils sedulously throughout the forenoon; bearing a hand, it may be, in the making or marring of some half-dozen fortunes. Then, at his club or elsewhere, he goes in for a lunch, 'free' in more senses than one, dallies perhaps a little with the big black cigar ensuing, and returns for another short spell at work. But little serious business is transacted after three in the afternoon. The rest of the day each man spends after his own devices. A drive on the Cliff House road behind a fast team, is perhaps the favourite amusement, although many indulge in less healthful recreations ; but, howsoever their other tastes may differ, almost all these capitalists thoroughly understand the theory and practice of dining. The *cuisine* of San Francisco is truly meritorious. If the number of the dishes be limited, for the purveying of a toothsome banquet, to say nothing of the difference in cost, I will back mine honest host of the 'California' against Delmonico of world-wide fame. A certain *salmi de grenouilles. à l'Espagnole* will, I wot, live long in more gastric memories than mine. During the evening, often till night has far waned, both at the clubs and in private houses there is much prevalence of 'Poker.'

Forasmuch as this famous game, more than any other with which I am acquainted, illustrates a national character, a few words may be specially devoted to it here.

The salient if not the best points in the American temperament are, perhaps, coolness of nerve, keen perception of chances, and equanimity under either fortune—exaggerated in Southern recklessness. Now, of these qualities 'Poker' is the very touchstone.

The principles of the game are simple enough. Six players can compete ; but, in the last case, the pack hardly holds out, and five make the pleasantest table. Five cards are dealt to each player, and any or all of these may be exchanged for others from the 'deck' or *talon*. The rules differ slightly in the East and West ; but, usually, the strongest hand is a 'sequence flush' or *quint*—a *quint-major*, of course, strongest of all ; next to this come four aces, &c., then a 'full hand'—three and a pair ; and so on, through a like descending scale. Any hand may be thrown up at once ; in which case no loss is incurred save by the player next to the dealer, who is obliged to 'ante' a trifling sum. After the discard, commences a kind of Brag. Each player, in turn, has the option of raising the stake on his adversaries ; these may either accept the same, showing their hand, or 'bluff' with a yet higher, or retire at a sacrifice of all they have contributed to the pool. I purposely omit certain *minutiæ*, such as 'straddling,' raising before discard, &c.; but, from this shadowy sketch of the game, you may infer that it is no mean test of character. When its devotees affirm that a finished Poker-player must needs shine in any career, where tact, courage, and study of human nature are more essential to success than mere plodding industry, they do not, apparently, far outrun the truth.

Speech goes for nothing; for Poker-language is not only always parliamentary, but intended expressly to mislead and mystify: therefore, skill in physiognomy is most valuable, though even this must frequently be liable to err. Broad-leafed hats, drawn low over the brows, and even green shades, have been used to baffle scrutiny; but the real artist holds such shifts and subterfuges in utter scorn. In strait ever so sore, his trained eyes neither lower nor lighten; over the fourth ace or the sequence complete, his cheek never flushes; and, bluffing on the weakest of pairs, he would betray not so much emotion as Hugo imputes to our great Marshal, when, at the turn of the battle—*Le Duc de Fer ne sourcilla pas; mais ses lèvres blêmirent.* But such men *nascuntur, non fiunt*; and no amount of practice, unsupported by natural qualifications, will produce the perfect exemplar.

Extreme caution is almost as fatal a fault as extreme audacity; and the player, who ventures only on strength, will rarely draw a remunerative pool; for his crafty opponents read his hand like a book, and the very 'ante's' will break him at last. A well-garnished purse is, of course, a very shield and buckler; for the stakes must needs be made in money or notes: unless by special agreement no bluffing on parole, or I O. U.'s, are allowed. A story I heard, years ago, illustrates this rule rather happily.

It was in the palmy days of the Mississippi, when the South was full of coin and courage; and you may fancy the 'plunging' on board the floating palaces in which the rich planters went to and fro. A small confederacy made large profits by working in this wise. They lay in wait for a big pool, and then 'raised' with a stake that it was next to impossible the wealthiest traveller could cover in cash: by the Mississippi rule, cheques were not a legal tender, and borrowing from outsiders was prohibited. This stake was their entire capital; and, for a long time it remained intact, whilst on the interest thus accruing the speculators lived royally ; changing their quarters often, so as to avert suspicion. On a certain day the gang confronted a solitary opponent—a staid, elderly person, who had sat down only under protest, and after long solicitation. At the proper crisis, the chief gambler produced the famous pocket-book.

"I go 20,000 dollars higher," he said ; "and you've five minutes to cover."

The countenance of the decent elder fell blankly. In great dudgeon, he remonstrated against such a violation of the spirit of the game, and appealed to the bystanders ; but all availed nothing, and the time of grace was waning fast. The gambler was beginning to gather the pool, when, with a sigh like a groan, the patriarch unbuttoned his vest, and from a chain round his neck detached a mighty wallet, by the side of which the other note-case was as a lady's *porte-feuille.* From its recesses packet after packet, roll after roll, of good bank-paper emerged.

"I go 100,000 better," he said ; "and you've five minutes to cover."

The defeat was simply crushing ; for, besides a few dollars of petty cash, it left the confederates penniless: but they accepted it with that wonderful fortitude which redeems some of the basenesses of the trade. Did they wax wroth, I wonder, a week later, when they discovered that their conqueror was no other than the cashier of one of the chief banks in New Orleans, carrying down supplies to one of its branches?

Though from the 'raise' being limited to ten dollars, there is less scope here for splendid audacity than for cool science, at that same Pacific Club are found some of the most famous players west of Chicago. Often and often, arriving late when the table was full, I have watched the game with no less interest than if it had been a crack rubber at the 'Portland.' I did not witness any of the big gambling bouts, with which certain Californian magnates beguile their brief leisure and lighten their plethoric purses. At one of these, shortly before our arrival, a celebrated Pioneer won close on forty thousand pounds sterling; and drew every cent of his winnings before noon of the day on which the thirty-six hours' sitting broke up.

After all, without crossing the Atlantic, you will never understand the wonderful hold of this game on all classes of American society. Judges on circuit, and even grave divines, are said sometimes to succumb to its fascination ; about the heaviest Poker in all the States flourishes in the shadow of the Capitol; as for the miners, if you would know how deeply their thoughts, dreams, and daily talk are imbued with its spirit, you have but to read Bret Harte.

Finally, now that you are probably weary of the subject, I have done it but scant justice.

CHAPTER VII.

The following Saturday found us on the rail running betwixt the uttermost spurs of the Santa Cruz Sierra and the bay of San José. Anyone, ever so slightly acquainted with Franciscan society, will guess whither we were bound; indeed, our host's hospitality has become so completely an 'institution,' that it is needless to name him.

It was a pleasant journey—none the less so, because a Maryland face was found in our company. When I looked on it last, the kindly lips would have set themselves like stone rather than have smiled on one of the 'Northern scum.' But in nine years many changes are rung; and, if the fair dame has 'bated somewhat of her prejudices since she vowed to honour and obey yonder doughty commander—presently Indian-taming in Arizona—she has but followed elder and wiser examples. Truly, it is best so. Why stir the soil above buried hatchets? So we talked of old times, and old friends, and old enemies to boot, with a sober historical interest. Only I was faintly sensible of an incongruity when, a few days later, under her auspices, we made acquaintance with the genial soldiers garrisoning Fort Presidio.

I have never seen anything at all resembling the *château* whither we were bound; but its plan seems well adapted to any climate where perfect ventilation is of more consequence than defence against cold. A broad, high gallery, provided with all imaginable couches and lounging-chairs, girdles three sides of a square, two-storied mansion. On the ground-floor are the living apartments, including a ball-room; on the second are the sleeping chambers, in which four-score guests have been sheltered ere now; and, everywhere, there is the same wealth of space and liberality of air and light. The great charm of the place is the absolute free-agency prevailing there. You are not bound to amuse yourself by rule, or, unless it seem good to you, to be amused at all. When the cheery host, as you enter his door, bids you—"Call for what you want, and do as you like,"—you feel that it is no form of words, and, if you are wise, act accordingly.

After dinner we all went to inspect the stables. These, like the house, are built entirely of wood, and, though brilliantly lighted with gas, were just as faultless in ventilation. More than fifty stalls were filled with a rare level lot of harness cattle, showing, with no deficiency of blood, an amount of substance rare even in a Californian stud, where good backs and loins are not, as in the East, an exception to the rule. Without a single celebrity among them, each and every animal standing there —barring a few young ones hardly furnished yet —looked, and I believe was, game to take its share in long, fast work. In truth, though a kind horse-master, our host drives after the manner of the son of Nimshi: however, a team of four, that can go up to '3.20,' satisfies even his requirements. A buyer rather than a breeder, he is justly proud of some of his deals; and it was my good luck to pick out the very apple of his eye—a slashing chestnut four-year-old, that looked like carrying fifteen stone alongside of any pack over any country.

In the carriage-houses, almost every form of vehicle, from the roomiest break to the flimsiest spider-waggon, was represented; indeed, I cannot remember another establishment where the old vaunt of—'Bring some more curricles'—could be so easily fulfilled.

Though the billiard-room lamps were burning far into the small hours, certain intrepid sight-seers were afoot soon after dawn; and, under convoy of our host, drove into the heart of the green hills that bound the horizon towards the west. They returned in a fine frame of scenic enthusiasm; but, for reasons good, my mate and I were fain to take their raptures on trust. However, we were to have our own picturesque experiences; for the digestive cigar, following a long late breakfast, was scarcely consumed, when our host was on the box of his break again--brisk, bustling, and energetic, as though he had just issued from his bed-chamber, instead of having steered a pulling team over a score of miles of cross-country road, abounding in steep pitches, soft places, and awkward angles.

I suppose that nowhere, outside the tropics, could be found a more marvellous variety of vegetation than these lowlands, and the adjoining slopes, display. Every tree, shrub, and flower indigenous to the region, and many exotics to boot, seem to flourish kindly here; and, ever and anon, over the tender green and vivid emerald of the recent plantations, or over the gay garden-broideries, towers a huge holm-oak—writhen, gnarled, and grey as the legendary Italian olives—like a Pict giant among the Scots.

We drove through the grounds of two or three country seats that afternoon: standing amongst the shaven lawns and trim *parterres* of one of these, you might have fancied yourself at Roehampton. The stables too were a picture in their way; though they wore a gaudy look to an English eye, and much varnish and plated work might have been dispensed with. I saw the like luxury of ornament during the War, at poor Will Macdonald's stud-farm near Baltimore; but in the box thus bedizened stood Flora Temple—queen of the trotting turf, whose 'time' was then unrivalled. The owner of this *buen retiro* is a man of mark, even here where financial celebrities are rife; and his history is a fair type of the country and period.

A few years ago he was a struggling storekeeper, with a small share in a small mine; and, once, was fain to send away his customers empty-handed, because his credit was not good for a sack of corn. He struck a 'good lead' at last, and came to San Francisco with more than a moderate competence. But the dogged courage, hopeful energy, and straightforward common sense, which had thriven in the hills, went astray in the crooked ways of California Street; and, within a brief space, a huge cantle of his pile melted, like a spring snowball, in the grasp of the broking guild. Now, somewhere up in Silverland, there was being worked a certain mine, more modest in its promises than in its requirements; for, if the dividends were irregular and rare, the 'calls' came like clock-work. As a natural consequence the value of the stock slid downwards, till at last it stood nominally at three dollars a share, but was scarcely quoted on 'Change. To the manager of this property the speculator aforesaid had once shown no small kindness; and thus the other requited it. For some time past, he had been exploring on his own account; working only with men whom he could trust not to reveal the results to outsiders, or even to their fellows. When he was prepared to show some thirty thousand dollars' worth of exposed ore, he hastened down to San Francisco. The whole twelve thousand shares might be bought up for thirty-six thousand dollars; would his friend find the money? It was a heavy—a very heavy—pull. If this venture went awry, there was an end to leisure and ease, and nothing for it but the precarious toilsome hill-life all over again; but this man had faith in his comrade, and the pluck of that famous hazard-player who, when the dice were most unkind, would cry, smiling—"In spite of our late losses and reverses, the main will still be Seven." Before the following night, Mr. H—— controlled all this stock, in which he was already largely interested, at the aforesaid price. When we were in San Francisco the market value of each share was seven hundred dollars—very few being procurable at that price; and the monthly profits of the mine were over half a million.

So if this honest *magnifico* should elect to have stable-fittings of virgin silver, or to pace to and fro, amongst his roses and Calla lilies, on emerald velvet instead of on soft lawn turf, he might safely please his fancy; and, I believe, none, howsoever they may have envied, begrudged him his good fortune.

Whilst we are on the subject, it is worth while remembering that a curious fatality seems to attach to these ventures. The cases are rare indeed, where the original discoverers of the richest claims have profited largely thereby. An instance, quoted by Mark Twain, is substantially correct, and has many parallels. "The owner of two-thirds of the Gould and Curry mine sold out for two thousand five hundred dollars, and an old horse, that ate up his value in seventeen days; whilst his partner—even less provident—traded for Government blankets and 'tangle-foot' whisky. Four years later, the market value of the property exceeded seven millions in gold coin."

Though you know of a surety that things have gone so, when, passing out of the presence of one of these prosperous magnates, you encounter a woful, haggard creature—unkempt, unwashed, questing for drink like a dry-lipped hound—it is hard to realise that the two can ever have started fair in the same race, and had even chances in the great Lucky Bag wherein all, save a few special favourites, must dive blindfolded. Nevertheless, it may well have been thus; and the contrast should suggest no light warning.

The drive homewards, winding through the spurs of the hills, was wonderfully picturesque; and, by rare good luck, the tide was high in the bay; so that, looking seaward, you saw no sour salt marshes or sullen mud-flats, but only the ἀνήριθμον γέλασμα of rippling sun-lit waters.

After the parting *skäl*, a fresh team rattled us down to the station. Whilst we waited for a train, one of our party, fond of statistics, amused himself by computing how many horses had been harnessed for our special behoof since dawn. Thirty-four was the sum of the addition—not a bad average for a Day of Rest.

CHAPTER VIII.

I HAVE heard Californians aver that, when travelling or residing in other lands, a certain insipidity in the surroundings soon turned the current of their desires back towards their 'ain countrie.' Allowing somewhat for provincial vanity, there may be much truth in this; at any rate, Franciscan life has a wonderful fascination for most strangers. Not the fascination of idleness or ἀκολασία; for the city resembles ancient Sybaris no more than it does ancient Athens; and a thorough epicurean would be as much misplaced here as any other philosophic dreamer. There are strangely few drones in this vast part-coloured hive; and to almost every male adult each day brings its tale of work, whether of head or hand.

It is not a soil wherein the Sciences, grave or gay, or the Fine Arts, are likely specially to thrive. Though a cunning painter will not lack patrons, and sweet singers, coming from afar, may count on hearty welcome and rich guerdon, probably in no other city in the United States is the consumption of literature, even of the lightest, so small. I heard a Franciscan of mark confess, half regretfully, that he could never find time for reading except in the railway-cars; and, doubtless, he might have spoken for many of his fellows. A tinge of bustle and business mingles with their Sabine leisure; and, even in his country-house, the romance must be daintily seasoned that would chain a true Californian to his chair for a stricken hour. A book-worm is a rarity such as no Western museum can show. There is no dearth of schools and colleges; and useful, if not liberal, education permeates very far down in the social scale; but, I imagine, the studies of the rising generation have for the most part some practical end; and the dead languages are rather lightly entreated in the politest of these academies.

You meet with rare exceptions—men like Judge H——; who has Horace at his fingers' ends, and will stray as far as you please through metaphysical mazes; but this amiable and erudite person, despite his patriotism, would subscribe to much that is set down here, and regarded himself, intellectually speaking, as rather a castaway.

Yet they are a pleasant folk to consort with, these jovial plutocrats. Though 'rough diamonds' are not uncommon, you will very seldom encounter the purse-pride or assumption of the *parvenu*; and 'shoddy' is at a discount here. Moreover, in outward seeming, they differ widely from their compeers on the Eastern shore. Most of the faces you meet, as you drive along the Cliff House road, wear the healthy tan of sun and sea breeze; and most of the frequenters of California Street look as if they could yet do a good day's work, if need were, up in the hills. In fine, the influences of the place, social as well as physical, are decidedly bracing.

The Cliff House reminds me of another Franciscan *spécialité*. In no other city, in either hemisphere, do such teams stand for daily hire. The keeper of one livery stable is generally open, I believe, to bet that he will produce thirty machiners that will do their mile in a few seconds over three minutes, trotting to the pole. Out of more than one pair, both Tressilian and myself could get '2.50,' without great pressing; and, under hands that they were accustomed to, the time might, doubtless, have been much improved. Some of the private teams are very remarkable: one, belonging to a principal banker, I shall remember as the perfection of its kind.

A pair of dark brown mares, own sisters, and the most marvellous match in colour, shape, and action; standing just 15.3; clean-limbed, large-eyed, lean-headed, as red hinds, with plenty of substance—they made a picture that, set before any lover of horse-flesh, must play havoc with the Tenth Commandment. Being under seven, they had scarce, according to American notions, come to their prime; but twice, driven by their owner—a fair, though hardly a first-class whip—we timed them over the mile track at the Agricultural Park under 2.35. The Commodore—an authority in such matters—guessed that in New York they would be cheap at twenty-five thousand dollars; and I still hold them peerless, after reviewing all the celebrities of Haarlem Lane.

Neither money nor pains are spared to produce these fast cattle; but, beyond question, the climate and pasturage are all in favour of the breeder. There are not a few cases even of aged horses, brought hither from the East, whose turn of speed has improved surprisingly.

Notwithstanding all this, the charioteering facilities at San Francisco are, in some respects, limited. The two avenues to the Pacific, mentioned above, are literally the only roads available for an afternoon-drive; and, before you emerge on either of these, you must needs rattle over uneven pavement and creaking planks, lined and interlined by the tramways of the street-cars. These last are, doubtless, most commendable institutions for cheapness and utility; but, contemplated from a coaching point of view, they are an utter offence and abomination.

At a Greenwich dinner last summer, I listened to some strong opinions concerning the latest improvements in our southern suburbs; and then I wondered how those ill-used dragsmen would have spoken, had they been confronted, daily and hourly, with the iron network compassing this city like a shirt of mail. 'Cater' across the rails ever so cleverly, you cannot escape jolt and jar; and, with the slightest divergence from the track when the wheels are fairly in the groove, comes a prolonged grating wrench, recalling dental memories. How some of the slender, fragile-looking vehicles escaped constant dislocation, was a puzzle to our

British minds, even after visiting Kimball's famous factory. These cunning artificers seem to have worked out the problem, of combining strength and durability with incredible lightness of draught, to the very last figure. They built for the Commodore a spider-waggon, weighing just 90 lbs., pole included; and to this conveyance, drawn by a fast team, he would entrust over fourteen stone of very solid flesh with perfect confidence—no mean test of tough hickory and hardened steel.

The extreme looseness and friability of the soil, in many places little better than shifting sand, must try the skill and patience of the engineer; but solid metalling and secure fencing are, as has been proved here already, simply questions of expense; and I affirm that the present state of the land-approaches to San Francisco is a stain on Western civilisation. Take, for instance, the road trending southwards into the heart of San Mateo county, along the shore of the San José Bay. This is a main highway, passing through a country well populated and fertile to a degree; all along it lie the country seats of bankers, merchants, and mining magnates—men of mark and means, not wont to count the cost when comfort or convenience are in question. Let me give a personal experience thereof.

Threading the suburbs, you are prepared, of course, for incessant tramways and much dodging of street-cars, also for the succession of long wooden bridges spanning marshy tidal inlets ; but the piece of road ensuing would, to most strangers, be rather a surprise. Imagine a long bare causeway—without a curb or rim of earth to turn a wheel, let alone an attempt at fence or parapet,—falling away on either hand, till about midway you look down into hollows some thirty feet deep, strewn with rugged boulders. Down the centre run the inevitable rails ; and as the car—rather larger than those plying in our suburbs—overlaps these, there is barely room, by drawing aside, to let it pass. Further, imagine your near-side horse somewhat shy and raw, and apt to hang heavily on the pole at any encounter with these infernal machines. At the very tightest point of the *Via Mala*, your enemy emerges from a cutting ahead, and bears down on you at a steady implacable trot. Would you fancy the position? The subscriber did *not*, he is free to allow ; and his misgivings seemed to find an echo in the breast of his comrade—no other than 'Dick,' the merry mystifier of Salt Lake City. We shaved by somehow; but betwixt the off-wheel (they pass here by the Continental rule) and the causeway's verge I doubt if two dollars would have lain flatwise. The rest of the road, in parts lapped by the wavelets of the Bay, is most attractive, and, save on the darkest night, quite devoid of peril. Also, there are some rare stretches of trotting ground; and we passed the seventeenth milestone in just a hundred minutes from the door of the Grand Hotel. But in a score of places, at least, we were fain to pick our way carefully to avoid hole or quagmire; though, for weeks past, not a rain-cloud had flecked the sky.

Such a trivial incident would not be worth recording, were it not, to some extent, illustrative of a feature in the Californian *morale*. Despite of regular business habits and professional caution, some of the sober city folk, when once clear of commercial trammels, evince a carelessness of life and limb worthy of a mining camp. When this road—much the shortest and easiest, albeit not the sole approach to San Francisco—might have been made secure for a few hundred dollars, and solid for a few thousand more, that a merchant-prince, such as our entertainer of that day, should travel it contentedly in its present state, seemed an anomaly not less strange than would be highwaymen on modernised Hounslow Heath.

Without the attraction of a sumptuous banquet, the mansion itself would have been well worth a visit. From almost every window the eye might rest on a landscape, scarcely less attractive than the master-pieces of Bierstadt adorning the inner walls; and the specimens of polished woods—notably in one room, panelled from floor to ceiling with blended shades of mountain laurel—were quite a study. The very place wherein to lounge away a calm bright afternoon; and only the recollection of the 'bad bit' aforesaid made us turn citywards again, before the sun was low.

More pleasant hours we spent at Fort Presidio, the district head-quarters of artillery. The position, as a matter of course, commands the Bay; the defences of which are so nearly complete as to render forcible entrance next to impossible. But few grim evidences of war are visible here; and there will be fewer yet ere long, if the project of converting a wide *plateau* of waste land, just without the lines, into a people's park be carried into effect. The officers' quarters contrast strangely with our notions of barrack. accommodation in the provinces. Instead of a couple of dull scanty rooms, opening on to a common stair, the wife even of a subaltern can count on a neat, semi-detached house, looking over a trim grassplat in front and a garden to the rear, with vines and creepers to the eaves for the mere trouble of training. The American system of 'roster,' at least in this branch of the service, differs materially from ours. A battery appears, not unfrequently, to remain for years at the same station: so no wonder that the nests of some of these warlike birds are so comfortably feathered, and that

> Securely there they build, and there
> Securely hatch their young.

One of the field-officers at Fort Presidio is a hunter of great renown; and from him I learnt much concerning the sporting capabilities of the country. Quails—much larger and handsomer birds, especially the mountain variety, than ours—seem to abound almost everywhere; and on the hills, within a short hour's sail of the fort, on the opposite side of the Bay, a fair shot and staunch walker would rarely return empty-handed from a stalk after deer. The snipe and wild-fowl shooting on the rivers and marshes draining into Benicia Bay sounds very tempting; but it could only be properly worked from a small yacht, or, better still, a large steam launch of light draught; and in an inclement season, like the last, success is, at the best, uncertain. The farther afield you go southwards, the better seem the chances of sport, particularly amongst the big game; and in the vast *ranches* lying betwixt the Pacific and the sierras of Santa Barbara, Los Angeles, and San Diego, you may come to as close quarters as may please you with veritable 'grizzlies.'

Even so far west as this, most shooting men, who can afford it, though they use the home-made rifle, affect the British breechloader; and all the Major's dogs were of pure English breed, if not directly imported. One brace of black and tan setters—a recent acquisition—were handsome enough to have taken a prize at any show. Their owner vouched them as good as they looked; and, though we could not try them actually on game, better form of galloping I have seldom seen on Scottish moors.

A visit to the Chinamen in their own quarter, was a necessity. Knowing that they thrive not ill, and seem tolerably content with their lot one is yet moved to compassionate the meek, laborious aliens—toiling, many of them, all their lives in a land so strange that none will leave his bones therein, if at any cost, or by stealth, they can be carried back to the Flowery Land. They are not often, in the cities at least, physically maltreated now; but they always wear a weary, overborne look, these poor Celestials; and a harsh word, or violent gesture, will make the boldest of them shrink like a dog, who, in the hands of the kindest master, never quite forgets his breaking. Though they can do almost any amount of certain kinds of work, there is something emasculate about the whole race, at least when transplanted here. Looking at their beardless faces, small hands, and slender limbs, it does not seem strange that they should be so apt at washing, cooking, and other household drudgery that in most countries falls to the women's share. Neither is this impression much weakened, even when you realise that a sullen implacability often underlies this outward submissiveness. I should be loth to make a friend of a Chinaman—still more loth to lie at his mercy as an enemy; but then the same remark might apply to divers classes of females, all the world over.

The Ghetto at Rome is—or used to be—a curious instance of isolation; but the Chinese quarter at San Francisco appears, in this respect, even more remarkable. Wheresoever his lines may fall, this incorrigible heathen clings to his native habits and observances with a touching fidelity; and it would be easier to wash a blackamoor white, than to argue or 'improve' him out of these. The first time we passed through the narrow noisome streets it was after dark; and the Sailor, who had been stationed for a year at Hongkong, averred that, without the slightest effort of imagination, he could have fancied himself in Canton again. From the recesses of the low-browed dens floated the faint, sickly odours of the incense-lights, burning before the Josses, mingled, ever and anon, with the deadlier savour of smouldering opium; the tiny coloured lanterns displayed the same quaint, old-fashioned wares, and abominations of victuals which, from time immemorial, have pleased the Celestial taste and palate; most of the shops, besides a placard in Barbarian language, bore a scroll inscribed with the well-known mystic characters; and the tradesmen, squatting within, reckoned up their gains and losses, not with pen and ledger, but with a kind of *abacus* of complicated beads and wires, by the aid of which a Chinese, even of the lower orders, will work out an intricate sum with a rapidity that would leave any ordinary book-keeper far behind.

I write the word ' noisome ' advisedly; for, though as a domestic, he is cleanly enough in his habits, ' John's ' warmest advocates—amongst the educated classes in America there is no lack of these—will hardly deny that, when cowering over his own hearth or mingling in a crowd of his fellows, he is a graveolent creature. Let any, who are sceptical of this, pay just one visit to his theatre at San Francisco. We were inducted there under fair and favourable auspices; and, albeit on escort duty, had special permission to smoke unlimited strong cigars. Well—before that night I never realised how nearly a savour may become substantial, and an atmosphere palpable. The heavy air seemed to cling round you, and work into your very garments like a Scotch mist; only, humidity was absent. It was impossible to define or classify the ill odours, as the poet did in

Cologne, town of ugly wenches.

Indeed, the subtle blending of infinite variety helped to make the whole effect so overpowering. Garlic did, perhaps, sometimes slightly predominate; but, before we could be sure of this, a narcotic whiff assailed the nostrils, and set our senses swimming. Where we were placed, there was elbow-room to spare, whereas the pit below was densely thronged; and there sit, nightly, for weeks together, the spectators of perhaps the dreariest pieces that have issued from civilised brains. For the Chinese playwright may be as prolix as he pleases, without fear of the 'cutting' that provoked placable Mr. Puff; and his public get their money's worth with a vengeance. It is not uncommon for a drama, embodying the history of some famous Emperor, or of a dynasty, to take some months of continuous representation. Fancy being compelled to sit it out—deafened, moreover, the while, by a running accompaniment of tom-toms, cymbals, and all manner of discord! Compared to this, surely it would be a light entertainment to study, line by line, those forty volumes of obsolete Italian history, to the perusal whereof a certain prisoner preferred the scaffold. Even with the help of an interpreter, it was difficult to pick up the slenderest thread of plot; especially as, when the situation seemed to be waxing at all impassioned or interesting, the orchestra was sure to strike in with a din drowning the dialogue: yet actors and actresses, to do them justice, spared not their lungs, and strained their voices to cracking. I have written 'actresses;' but I should be loth to swear to the sex of those strange beings, 'ruddled' till their faces shone again, gibbering and screaming there. The costumes were remarkable for profuse embroidery and violent contrasts of colour; but, had they been in better taste, they must have looked garish and tawdry on the ill-lighted stage. There was a good deal of sham fighting, but none of the combatants went through the form of smiting each other; neither was there any clashing of swords or bucklers. The whole affair seemed intended to display the feats of a few ordinary acrobats; and, very often,

Around them paused the battle,

whilst they flung somersaults, and otherwise contorted themselves.

The tenacity of purpose and powers of endurance, inherent in the sex, supported, it is probable, the matrons and maids of our company; for they had shown no signs of moving, when, on false pretext, I shame to say, of a forgotten business-engagement,

I fled and gat me out. The first gulp of fresh air—never very fresh, however, in that quarter—was like a cordial; but the cunningest drink that the Pacific steward could devise—availed not to wash out of my throat, that night, the *arrière-goût* of the Paynim.

Graver, if not wiser, heads than Bret Harte's, have been busy of late over the question of 'Chinese cheap labour;' and it is possible that the solution of many difficulties may be found here, notably of those now hampering the South.

A Chinaman would sooner lie down and starve, than delve underground for ever so liberal hire. Superstitious terrors lie, probably, at the root of this prejudice, which is insuperable. But of ordinary out-door labour he can do his fair share, supplying by neatness and assiduity the lack of physical power. An eminent railway engineer assured me that, in the long run, he could get more work out of a Chinese gang, controlled by a Chinese overseer or sub-contractor, than out of an equal number of Americans or Irish. Indeed, though, side by side with an ordinary navvy, 'John' looks but a puny atomy—burrowing on in mole-like fashion, he is pretty sure to complete the appointed task in the appointed time; whereas, with the other, broils, sprees, and strikes make this a very open question. Assuredly, in rivalry with the free negro, it seems long odds on pigtail against wool. In extremes of cold or wet, the 'Chinee' is apt to shrivel up and wax flaccid, and he has no nerve to fight against certain epidemics; but—opium being nearly his sole excess—he is rather a tough, than fragile, creature as a rule, and is like to thrive quite as well on a Louisiana cane-brake, or South Carolina rice-ground, as in his native paddy-fields.

There are, of course, certain inconveniences in dealing with people devoid of moral sense and moral dignity, who reckon lying and stealing amongst the Polite Arts; but the opportunities for the exercise of this last accomplishment, on an important scale, would be comparatively limited on a plantation; and a strict, not over-severe, supervision might do wonders. At any rate, the experiment seems worth trying, if it were only to bring the impracticable 'Pompey'—now absolutely master of the position—somewhat to his bearings. Some Southern landowners must be of this opinion; for the directors of more than one large steamship company have been sounded already as to the contract price of landing some thousands of coolies on that seaboard.

"San Francisco," writes Mark Twain, "a truly fascinating city to live in, is stately and handsome at a fair distance; but close at hand one notes that the architecture is mostly old-fashioned; many streets are made up of decaying, smoke-grimmed, wooden houses; and the barren sand-hills, towards the outskirts, obtrude themselves too prominently."

An impartial witness might further have recorded, the remarkable absence of any artificial shade. Not that even on the sand-hills, encompassing the city, it is 'barren all;' for, where there is shelter from the sea-winds, there is wealth of vegetation: but it is vegetation—not woodland. There are orchards and vines, of course; but, with the exception of a few tall shrubs in Woodward's Gardens, you may go far afield beyond the extremest suburbs, before you find anything resembling a forest tree. However, if your soul thirsts for umbrage, you have but to take the steam-ferry across the Bay to Oakland, where there is no lack of greenery, great and small.

Of this, her rival, San Francisco is waxing exceeding jealous; and, it would seem, with reason good. A few years ago, it was a mere group of isolated villas, owned by wealthy citizens, with semi-rural tastes. Nowadays, a densely populated town stretches landward from the Central Pacific Terminus; whilst on its outskirts imposing frame-houses, and more substantial edifices, are springing up daily; and the price of building lots has risen fabulously. It is, indeed, a very pleasant place of sojourn; for, when the waters within the Golden Gate are all a-foam, the sea-winds breathe gently here, even if they are not held wholly at bay by the hill-rampart to the north-west, over which Monte Diablo looms like a keep.

Nevertheless, the residential attractions of Oakland will, probably, ere long, be merged in its commercial importance. Whether the Goat Island project has been carried out or no, I cannot say. On this barren islet, lying nearly midway betwixt the City and their present Terminus, the Central Pacific Company proposed to build a vast depôt; bridging over the shallows dividing it from the mainland. The bill was strongly opposed—not in San Francisco alone, where conflict of interest was evident, but by strategists, who argued that the occupation of this point by Government was absolutely necessary to the complete defence of the Bay. If the bill should pass, it is not difficult to foresee the effect. The want of unbroken land-communication has already told heavily on the commerce of the City; and, if the goods traffic were still more powerfully concentrated at Oakland, the balance of mercantile power would be turned in earnest—presently, at least. For, ere the world is much older, the last links of a double or triple chain, knitting San Francisco to the South-East will certainly be welded.

CHAPTER IX.

The most attractive, if not the most important, thoroughfare in San Francisco is Montgomery Street; and chief, beyond doubt, of the temptations that here beset the stranger, is the Photographic Gallery. At the proper season, the atmospheric conditions seem specially favourable to the process, and the results are very remarkable. Though this branch of art has so marvellously advanced of late, the views of the Yosemite Valley might, I think, challenge European comparison.

> The swan upon St. Mary's lake
> Floats double, swan and shadow,

writes Wordsworth. Would not the 'gentle lover of nature' have rhymed to some purpose, if he had seen a whole mountain-side so exactly reflected in a vast crystal mirror, that at the first glance it is hard to discern where rock merges into water? This effect the cunning worker in collodion has reproduced with absolute fidelity. I should like to know—not intimately, but at a respectful distance—the traveller who would issue from those seductive saloons with unloosened purse-strings.

The very mention of Californian landscape draws English thoughts towards Arnold Bierstadt; and the great painter has honour in his own country, no less than in ours. I shall not lightly forget a forenoon spent in his studio; or the patience and courtesy which enabled us to exhaust, to the last tiny scrap, portfolios crammed with sketches in water-colour. In the depths of this last winter he had succeeded in reaching the Yosemite Valley—a feat of which the Alpine Club might have been proud; although he himself made so little of it, that only from our own experience, and the hints of native mountaineers, could we guess at the risks and privations that must need have been incurred. Almost all the recent drawings were mere studies; but one or two stormy sunsets were marvels of weird light and shade; and you could not look narrowly into the crudest of them without perceiving how it might work into some corner of a noble picture. Throughout, there was the same delicate touch and soft elaboration of detail; and—speaking not *ex cathedrâ*—I take leave to doubt if, since Claude Lorraine, any have rivalled Bierstadt in the handling of gnarled trunk, twining creeper, or feathery spray.

A view of the Donner Lake in oils, from a point adjacent to the Central Pacific Railway, was nearly complete ; and on the easel rested a half-finished picture of the Seal Rocks. Even thus, this last was well worth lingering over. The slow swash of the Pacific surge, with its creamy foam-fringe, just sufficing to lift the lazy sea-lion on to his rocky pillow, was simply perfect ; and some cavernous clefts, half veiled by broken water, were miracles of *chiar-oscuro*.

In about a fortnight the 'Arlington' brought down the rest of our company, safe and sound, but very weary and travel-stained. And then we knew that our days here were numbered, and that whatsoever of business or pleasure was on hand, behoved to be done quickly. Our comrades had not altogether wasted time and trouble, having, indeed, seen much to reward prospecting ; but the same stumbling-block noted above—want of development —they had met with almost everywhere. Not that this in any wise checks the tide of speculation, but rather amplifies and accelerates it.

Perhaps it would be hard to find a Yorkshireman, owning or tilling a hundred acres of land, without a horse to sell; but, trust me, it would be infinitely harder to light on a Californian of means—not that this condition is indispensable—without a mine, or a moiety thereof, at the disposal of the first likely customer. And, though you be palpably an uncommercial traveller—howsoever warlike, learned, or reverend be the calling of your interlocutor—I would not insure you against temptation for a 'red cent.'

Tressilian having, despite his constant disclaimers, a certain reputation as a capitalist, was a tempting quarry. A deer turned out at Salt Hill may give you some faint idea of how he was mobbed and hunted; and I always wondered that he did not oftener turn to bay. When he arrived at San Francisco he was suffering from the effects of a heavy fall in a Calaveras prairie; his mustang having come down headlong when going at top speed. A leading physician of the city—personally known, besides, to one of our company—was summoned, and soon ascertained that no serious harm was done. A very reverend signor: not exactly simple-looking; but, with his long white hair and grave weary eyes, most guileless in outward seeming—the kind of man you would fancy too locked up in his profession to be well versed in the world's ways. When, one evening just before the dinner-hour, we saw the tall, spare figure, with bent head, crossing the *carrefour* under our windows, both the Commodore and I opined that the doctor's errand was to inquire after, or perhaps inspect, his patient.

"But," said Tressilian, "I'll take twenty dollars to ten, that he has got a mine in his pocket."

The bet was booked; and, for once, the Commodore's astuteness was at fault. Having required a private interview, from the recesses of his long-skirted garment the sage produced not one, but a brace of these ventures, with the shadowy outlines of a third.

For myself, I began to have 'lodes' and 'pockets' on the brain; and, in the still watches of the night fancied that low voices were murmuring of millions: it was as though I were haunted by the spirit of some luckless speculator, drowned, long ago in the seething silver whirlpool. Not the least amongst the advantages of the Pacific Club was its immunity from this annoyance. Mining topics could not have been intentionally tabooed; yet I cannot remember hearing them more than casually alluded to, even by those who came in 'red-handed' from the battle on 'Change. 'Battle' is scarcely a misnomer; for nowhere else, perhaps, within the scope of mercantile speculation, might be seen such desperate onslaughts, such wily ambushments, such ruthlessness of victory, such woe to the vanquished.

Perhaps intense weariness of the whole subject, not less than natural proclivities and force of old association, turned my own thoughts and inquiries into another channel—whereof more anon.

Our experiences of San Francisco were fast drawing to a close; but one we lacked yet; and this void the Sailor took not a little to heart.

"We've never had our earthquake yet," he used to remark, mildly, but querulously; just as one might speak of an 'unavoidable,' omission, in the programme of a new opera.

I argued that it was extremely improbable that a city, perfect hitherto in hospitality, would send a stranger away, even on this point discontented. Nevertheless, our comrade did so depart —preceding the rest by some three days or so, with the view of visiting the Big Trees in Calaveras and rejoining us *en route.*

On the night but one ensuing—or rather on the third morning, for the hour was 'far ayont the twal'—I was walking home from the club up Montgomery Street, with one companion; a sojourner like myself, though of longer date, and also just flitting Eastwards. Suddenly, I was aware of a sensation new and strange—not a shock, but a kind of quiver, thrilling from the soles of the feet upwards; and, without quite staggering, I was fain to sway to and fro involuntarily. At the same instant the pavement grew unstable, not violently, but like a raft floating on a lake faintly wind-stirred; and the tall houses over against us—this was a mere optical delusion, of course—seemed to waver in the uncertain twilight.

Honestly conscious of sobriety—when we left the club the strictest martinet might have put either of us through our 'facings'—I could not guess what ailed me; and set it down, at first, to a dizziness or other passing disorder of the brain. But, glancing aside at my companion, I noticed that his right hand was propped on a convenient shop-rail as he stood stock still.

He had good cavalier blood in his veins, this gay Down-Easter: for generations past his family had kept up their connections with the old country; and he himself had visited it frequently. On the present occasion, he evinced an amount of phlegm worthy of that wonderful creation, the Englishman of the French drama. To be sure, he had been beaten twice or thrice that night on a 'full hand'; and a losing gamester, as all men know, cares neither for 'the devil nor the deep sea.' I have no reason to believe that his acquaintance with these phenomena was more extensive than my own; but he only shrugged his shoulders depreciatingly, muttering, "Pretty mean earthquake." And so marched on, musing, as before.

A very faint jar, immediately ensuing, was followed by absolute tranquillity; and, after waiting a minute or two, deeming the performance over, I followed my philosophic friend. But, thenceforth, I wondered no longer at wood replacing stone in so many of the imposing edifices within and around the city.

So slight a shock would scarce have troubled the slumbers of any true Franciscan. A few bells rang of their own sweet will; doors swung open in a ghostly fashion; and more crockery was broken than cats or clumsy fingers can usually account for: but there was no excuse for a panic, and nothing like general alarm.

However, the anger of the earth, which visited us so lightly, was felt in bitter earnest elsewhere. Throughout the south-western counties there was rack and ruin; and in San Bernardino nearly an entire village was swallowed up in a yawning chasm,—living souls going down into the pit, as in the 'gainsaying of Kore.' Even in Stockton our Sailor's rest was rudely broken. The shock there was thrice repeated, each time with increased violence; and, before the third had ceased to vibrate, through every corridor in the hotel streamed half-clad fugitives; whilst the street without was soon similarly crowded. One 'commercial'—the brotherhood is always prominent in such emergencies—specially distinguished himself by leaping out of a back window on to a huge skylight below. He escaped with life and limb, much scarified; but the smash will probably be 'immortal' in that hostelry.

After Franciscan hospitality was thus made *teres atque rotunda*, we had few chances of further testing it. Though none murmured when the marching-orders were issued, one or two, I think, of our party accepted them in the spirit of the old Plymouth doggrel ditty :—

> 'Though it's 'cording to rule,' says the sergeant,
> 'It *du* seem 'nation hard ;'
> And so *I* thought, who listened
> To the 'plaint of the Dockyard guard.

One farewell banquet at the 'California,' at which mine honest host surpassed himself—one farewell bout of 'poker' at the Pacific, more in good fellowship than in spirit of gambling—grips of brawny hands that set our fingers a-tingling ; and then, through the chilly dawn-light, the Commodore and I walked back to the 'Grand' to get our traps together, just in time to catch the ferry to Oakland. There the Arlington awaited us, ready yoked to the eastward-bound train, and not unwelcome with its curtained couches.

CHAPTER X.

Frequent disappointments had so damped the ardour of our explorers, that not without difficulty they were persuaded to turn aside from the direct route eastward to inspect certain hydraulic mines in Nevada county. Albeit unfit for mountaineering—for a heavy cough was still tormenting me—I rejoiced, at the time, that it was so decided. About this expedition there was no shade of difficulty or hardship ; and the delay was more than repaid by what we saw and heard.

Here I must needs crave space for some statistics ; for the subject is really important, and scarcely so well known as it deserves to be. At least I am free to confess that, a few months ago, I had not so much as heard of this branch of industry ; and it is probable that the most of those who have kept me company thus far are in like plight.

Ten years ago, M. Laur—an impartial, I believe, no less than a competent, witness, for he was a distinguished French engineer—stated confidently that the auriferous gravels, in extent and thickness, are the most important gold mines of California.* It is impossible to understand this, without enduring a brief geological lecture. Wherefore in patience possess your souls—it being premised that I advance no theories of my own; but am simply transcribing those of our Professor.

"It seems clear," writes this learned person, "that, at the close of the geological epoch just prior to the appearance of man upon the globe, the western slopes of the Sierra Nevada mountains—the Alps of California—were, below a certain horizon, covered by a vast spread of alluvium; owing its origin, probably, to the action of extensive glaciers, which have left evidences of their former presence everywhere in the higher Sierras. The glaciers furnished the transporting power that brought from above the fragments, which, by long

* De la production des Metaux Precieux en Californie. Paris, 1862.

continued action of running water, were worn into the smoothly rounded boulders, gravel, and sands forming the gold bearing alluviums. The melting of glaciers, as their lower skirts reached warmer zones, furnished the water for these ancient rivers; whose beds are now found at elevations far above the level of the present river-system, and whose courses are generally crossed by the valleys of our modern streams. This condition of things continued long enough to permit the accumulation of beds of gravel to a depth and extent unknown anywhere else in North America; and, if we speak of auriferous deposits, unequalled elsewhere in the world. Of the thickness of this accumulated material we have evidence, in numerous places where it has been protected from the action of subsequent denudation by a capping of volcanic materials. In such places it reaches a known thickness of more than five hundred feet. Usually, however, it has been denuded to one-half of this thickness—often less—and, in many regions, has been completely swept away.

"Subsequent to the glacial and alluvial epoch, to which the gold-bearing gravels are referred, there was a period of intense volcanic activity; the evidence of which is seen most conspicuously in the Table Mountains, so called, which are cappings of basalt forming highly characteristic ranges. In other parts of the State, and especially in Nevada county, the volcanic outpourings consisted of ashes and fragmentary materials, consolidated into heavy beds of volcanic mud, with fragments of scoria, tufa, and basalt; which are found accumulated to the east of Columbia Hill, in Nevada county, to the height of many hundreds of feet. Following the outpouring of the volcanic matter, there has evidently been an epoch of very active denudation by running water; which has broken up and removed the volcanic cappings, leaving them entire only here and there, as landmarks showing the ancient levels—sweeping away likewise vast areas of the old alluvium, and re-distributing it as secondary or shallow '*placers*' at lower levels.

"This denudation was probably consequent on the sudden disappearance of the vast system of glaciers which, up to that time, crowned the entire range of the Sierras with ice. It was greatly more energetic in the southern portion than in the northern, where the mass of ancient alluvium remaining is very much greater than it is in the former region. The extent of the ancient alluvium, as well as the energy of the power which produced and subsequently denuded it, becomes apparent on a study of the phenomena.

"These extensive deposits of gold attracted the attention of the early adventurers in California, and were called 'Hill Diggings'; but their real nature and significance were not at first fully understood; and, being generally much above any sources of water supply then available for washing, they received but little attention. Especially were they overlooked, whilst the spoils were available, drawn by no other means than the miner's pan, shovel, and pick, from the productive 'bars' of adjacent rivers, and from the rich 'gulches' where the gold lay open to the first comer, in a concentrated form.

"So complete was the removal of the ancient gravel in some of the southern counties, that the gold, left behind by its weight, lay upon the naked rock, covered by only a few inches of vegetable mould—as at Mokelumne Hill, where, in the limits of a single 'claim,' fifteen feet square, the precious metal, to the amount of fifty thousand dollars, has fallen to the share of a single adventurer."

In further disquisition the Professor waxes a trifle too professorial for unscientific auditors ; and, for the rest of the way, I am guided by the rougher, but equally safe leading-strings lent by practical hydraulic miners.

The alluvium aforesaid, in many cases, is found to rest in a perfectly well-defined channel—not harder to trace, when the superincumbent soil is removed, than any other of the dried-up water-courses, through which, æons ago, flowed rivers ancienter than Pison. These troughs, varying in width from four hundred to a thousand feet or so, are lined and floored by 'rim-rock' and 'bed-rock' of greenstone, granite, or serpentine; and, wheresoever these are revealed, howsoever hard the material, grooves and cavities mark the course of the current, and witness to the fury of its eddies. Chiefest of these primeval streams, is that known in Nevada as the 'Great Blue Lead.' It has been traced, beyond the possibility of doubt, for near a hundred miles ; though, sometimes, it will be needful literally to remove mountains before the channel is laid bare.

The bluish tint is, by common consent, considered characteristic of the richer portions of the gravel ;

but, according to the Professor, it has no necessary connection with the presence of gold. The deposit is invariably more valuable, and more toughly cemented, as it nears the 'bed-rock;' but the peculiar colour is due only to exemption from oxidising influences. When exposed to the action of the air and atmospheric water, it disappears; passing into a dull yellow, sometimes brilliantly streaked with purple and red.

It would be difficult, indeed, to estimate in figures the value of these reserves of gold; but experts have calculated that in the districts betwixt the South and Middle Yuba rivers, there is stored up more of the precious metal than the whole of California has produced since 1849. The French engineer, quoted above, estimates that in five hundred years that portion of the auriferous gravel in this district, which now lies within the reach of water, will not be completely washed away; and he sets the annual revenue, for the whole period, at over ten millions of dollars. These vast treasure-beds lay unnoticed and comparatively unknown, till the shallow *placers* in the ravines and river-beds were more or less completely exhausted. But, when bars and gulches began to fail, and it needed Chinese patience to work pan and rocker, men began to scan the ground more narrowly and farther afield: so, ere long, the secret of the hills was known. From the first it was evident, that only by the hydraulic or some equally economical process could so vast an amount of passive resistance be attacked with any prospect of remunerative success; but the proper application of this mechanical agent, was a problem solved only after large experience and many abortive trials.

The following conditions are involved :—

1st. The moving of the whole mass of auriferous gravel, whatever its depth, quite down to the 'bed-rock.'

2nd. The accomplishment of this by the action of water alone—human labour being confined to the application of the water, and to the preliminary preparation for its supply.

3rd. The disintegration of the conglomerated matter, as a part of the uninterrupted operation of the whole system.

4th. The saving of the gold, without interrupting the continued flow of water.

5th. The disposal of the accumulation resulting from the removal of such vast masses of gravel.

These conditions are, in practice, met by the following steps; and once again I quote, I hope correctly, my Professor.

The mining ground being selected, a tunnel, or 'open cut,' is projected from the nearest and most convenient ravine or river bank; so that, starting in the 'bed-rock' on the face of the ravine, or other selected point, it shall approach the centre of the gravel mass to be moved, at a gradient of about one in twenty-four to one in thirty-six. The dimensions of this tunnel are usually six feet in width by seven feet in height, sometimes wider; and, where possible, it is carried on the line of contact between the granite and the shales, for the greater ease of excavation. These tunnels vary in length from a few hundred feet to a mile; some of the longer consuming from two to seven years in driving, at a cost of from ten to sixty dollars per foot, varying with the character of the rock to be excavated. The end of the tunnel is designed to reach, beneath the under surface of the gravel, the centre or deepest part of the channel, at a point where a shaft or incline is sunk through the gravel until it intersects the tunnel. It obviously demands careful engineering to carry out works of such magnitude with the accuracy required; and, for the want of sufficient care or skill in this particular, years of costly labour and anxious expectation were wasted in the early history of these enterprises.

The object of this laborious exploration is obvious. The long tunnel becomes a 'sluice-way;' through the whole length of which 'sluice-boxes' are laid, at once to direct the stream and save the gold. For this purpose a trough of strong planks is placed in the tunnel, from three to four feet wide, and with sides high enough above the pavement to control the stream. The pavement is usually composed of blocks of wood six inches in thickness, cut across the grain of the wood, and so placed as to expose the ends of the blocks to the wear of the current. The wooden blocks are usually alternated with sections of stone pavement—the stones set endways. In the interstices, quicksilver is distributed; as much as two tons of this metal being required to charge a long sluice.

The water from the canal is brought by side 'flumes,' or aqueducts, to the head of the mining ground, with an elevation of two hundred to five hundred feet above the 'bed-rock'; and it is conveyed into the bottom of the mining claims by iron pipes, sometimes sustained on a strong incline of timbers. These pipes are of sheet iron of adequate strength, rivetted at the joints; and measure from twelve to twenty inches in diameter. They connect with a powerful apparatus of cast iron, provided with an universal joint to which the outlet or 'nozzle' is attached, ending in a steel ring for the delivery of the stream, which varies from four to eight inches in diameter. This apparatus is sometimes called a 'monitor.'

The banks of gravel are usually worked in two benches. The upper is never so rich as the lower; and, being also less firm, is worked away with greater rapidity. The lower section is much the most compact; and the stratum on the 'bed-rock,' being strongly cemented by sulphuret of iron and great pressure, resists even the full force of the water stream, until it has been loosened by gunpowder. For this purpose adits are driven on the 'bed-rock,' forty to seventy feet from the face of the bank, and a tunnel extended at right angles to some distance each side of the adit. In this tunnel a large quantity of gunpowder is placed, and fired at by a train laid from without. Thus the compact conglomerate is broken up, and the water rapidly completes the work.

Even from this rough sketch, it must be evident that water in these parts is a very precious commodity. At any cost it must be secured and assured; or all other cost and pains are wasted. More than five thousand miles of artificial 'ditches' have been laid already, representing twenty millions of dollars expended; and many of these are worked by companies paying good dividends. Fifteen cents for an inch of water sounds exorbitant, and this is about the average; but a miner's inch is rather liberal measurement. It varies in different districts: generally an opening of one inch high and twenty-four long, is made with a pressure of six inches, producing, as I am informed, an outflow of about 17,000 gallons in each twenty-four hours. You cannot wander a mile on the western slopes of the Nevadas, without encountering a dozen of these 'flumes,' clinging to the steep sides of *cañons*, flying across ravines on trestle-work—strong and tough as a chain-bridge, though at a little distance it looks built of pipe stems—gurgling along merrily under sunlight, or murmuring sullenly as they dive under ground; and, ever and anon, you come on a reservoir, enclosing half a valley within its massive dam, where the abundance of spring rains and melting snows is stored, and where, over the murky water, peer, by hundreds, the gaunt heads of the drowned pines.

It follows that, though a hydraulic mine may be worked provisionally, it cannot, except in very exceptional cases, be completed and insured against the accidents of seasons — or rather against inevitable drought—without considerable outlay. Nevertheless, the advantage of this system of working, compared with any former process, will be apparent from the following table. Taking a miner's wages at three dollars per day, the cost of handling a cubic yard of gravel is—

With the pan	$15.00
With the rocker	3.75
With the Long-Tom	.75
With the sluice	.34
With the hydraulic process	.10

Now, you have heard nearly enough to enable you to understand what we saw. Like Canning's clerical tormentor, quoted aforetime, I have endeavoured not to be tedious with—I doubt not—precisely the same result.*

* In working out these and other personal recollections, I have been much aided by comparing notes with a very sensible little volume—"Six Months in California," by J. G. Player-Frowd.

CHAPTER XI.

THROUGH Alameda and San Joaquin once more; past boundless corn-straths, waving now in deeper green billows—past meadows, broidered like a royal robe with blue, crimson, and gold—past orchards, heavy in bloom—to Sacramento, where the Sailor rejoined us, having accomplished a visit to the Big Trees in Calaveras very easily.

He did not seem to have been much overawed by the spectacle. Indeed, I fancy that the expectations of most travellers outsoar the reality, vast though it be. If any one of the giant brotherhood stood out quite isolated, the effect would be infinitely grand; but it seems impossible to take in, at one glance, the proportions of any that stand erect; unless you except a pair called 'the Sentinels'; and, after long ravages of storm or lightning, these retain scarcely the semblance of a forest tree.

But our comrade had been anything but disappointed with his earthquake. What we felt at San Francisco, must have been as nothing compared with the three-fold shock which startled Stockton from its slumbers; and the panic in the hotel, however absurd in the retrospect, did not appear wholly groundless.

Our car was cast loose at Colfax late in the afternoon; and here we recognised, regretfully, that we had left behind those names of rich Catalan ring—tinged, as it were, with the *sangre azul*—and were back again among the Creeks, Flats, Villes, and other designations trivial and dissonant. Hence, a darkling drive of some four leagues brought us to Nevada City, over roads, testing almost too hardly the endurance of those wonderful 'Carson' waggons.

It was not without its merits, the hostelry in which we found shelter. The bar-whisky was not instantaneously fatal; by careful steering it was possible to move undefiled through the *crachoirs* of the crowded common room; and the bed-chambers only offended the nostrils through innocence of fresh air. But, though the night was yet young when we arrived, our host declined to furnish us with food of any kind whatsoever; and those who chose not to go to rest fasting had to search for their supper through mud and rain. I remember encountering the like difficulty at wayside inns in the Upper Tyrol; but it seemed odd to be so stinted in the chief house of accommodation of a tolerably populous 'city.'

Early on the morrow, we drove out into the hills dividing Nevada from the South Yuba Valley. The collar-work for the first four miles or so, over roads literally ploughed up by the heavy drays, was something fearful; but our wiry teams faced it with indomitable gameness, and we reached table land at last.

Mark Twain, if I remember right, complains of the monotony and melancholy of Californian forests, contrasting them unfavourably with like landscapes in the East. We strangers, however, found nothing to cavil at, and much to admire, in the woodlands we traversed that breezy forenoon. Where on earth will you find a grander tree than the red pine, rising pillar-wise, with never a knot or excrescence to mar its smooth stateliness? Would you crave for more diversity of forest colour than is supplied by the feathery cedar, the solemn black-oak, the vivid green buckeye, and the *manzanita* shrub, with its soft grey foliage and rosy blossom? If so, you are harder to please than was our company. Under the summer drought, of course, all these may look dull and arid: one can but speak of things as one finds them.

The mine we had been invited to visit was in full work; and, leaving our waggons at the manager's hut, we descended by a steep slippery track into the hollow where the nearest 'washings' lay. The peculiar features of the scene as we rounded the last corner of cliff, could scarcely be produced by photograph, much less by word-painting.

It was difficult to believe that human force, unaided by earthquake or volcano, could have produced such hideous desolation. A whole hill side quarried away, would give no idea of it; for, there, may be observed a certain regularity and method of attack; here, the spot might have been ravaged by some of the fantastic fiends of Cornish legend and German 'folk-lore.' On the soil, seamed, torn, scarified, and bestrewn with boulders, the foot finds no level resting-place; the cliff-face displays no sloping shelves, nor smooth sheer descents, but only yawning rifts and chasms, and gibbous crags nodding to their fall; and, here and there, tower uncouth islets of gravel—their dusky sides streaked with dull red and blue—marking the level where was opened the first parallel in this cruel war against the Great Mother.

Some fifty yards or so from the base of the bank lay the 'monitor,' silent and still; for the order to 'cease firing' had been sent down a while ago, so that we strangers might witness the opening of the battery.

An innocent-looking engine enough; with its rude wooden lever, and muzzle not larger than that of a light field-piece, it looked as if it might furnish a douche of more than average power. Yet Nimrod, or Anak, or the most puissant creature that has ever drawn breath of life, standing before it, a second later, would have been swept away like a dry leaf before a gale. Without danger you may lay your finger on the jet at its issue: then you will be sensible not of rushing fluid, but of something smooth, compact, and seemingly substantial as polished marble; and you are made aware that the edge of Excalibur could never have cloven that thin grey column in twain.

With the turning of a handle came a savage hiss—a smothered crash, as the fierce stream smote its mark—then a rumble and rattle, as great clots and crusts from the cliff hurled themselves into the whirl of water beneath, to be swallowed by the greedy sluice-way. The mass, then operated on, was not of the toughest cement; but the heavy boulders imbedded therein, fared little better than the lighter compost, when the furious stream once had them in grip: thenceforth, they too were pressed into man's service; each helping, as it was swept down, to grind its comrades to powder.

"One thousand miner's inches," says my technical adviser, "are equal to over one hundred thousand cubic feet of water, per hour, constantly discharged against the face of the bank, under a pressure of from one hundred to two hundred pounds to the square inch, varying with the height of the column; and this 'monitor' is working at about two-thirds of that power."

The information—however valuable in itself—does not, I confess, minish my wonderment; and I stand there staring, just as stupidly as before, at the great grey cliff literally *melting* away, like a sugar-loaf under a heated jet. By the help of the wooden lever aforesaid, the engine can be worked easily and accurately as any *mitrailleuse*; and, on inanimate matter, must be infinitely more fatal. It is part and parcel, I suppose, of our unregenerate nature to find an attraction in any grand spectacle of destruction. Why, otherwise, do we find sober and benevolent people watching a terrible fire or flood, with interest keener than that excited by the most moving melodrama? Howsoever profitable the ultimate result, there could be no question as to the present destructiveness of the process we were witnessing. This, therefore, may account for our reluctance in quitting it—even when made aware that time was pressing, if we would visit all we had come to see.

For some distance we followed the downward course of the sluice-way; clambering warily along slippery tracks, and passing gingerly over bare single planks, supported, athwart chasms disagreeably broad and deep, on unsteady trestles; and, as we went along, our conductors explained to us what work was carrying on—surely, though so swiftly—in the turbid torrent beneath.

The complete trituration of the gravel and other raw material is the prime essential. The action of impetuous water on the *débris* swept down is aided by a series of small cataracts—'dumps,' in mining parlance—at each of which the process of comminution is carried forward till the lowest level is reached, at a distance of half a mile or more from the first fall. The internal preparation of the sluice-way has been described above; but it is difficult to realise that, under all this turmoil and hurly-burly, the quicksilver is quietly absorbing the minutest particle of gold into a brittle amalgam. Yet, rude as this method may appear, experience has proved that more gold is saved thereby than by any method of washing yet devised; whilst, in point of economy, no comparison can be made. At intervals of from fifteen to thirty days, according to the extent of the operation, and the richness of the material worked, comes the 'cleaning up;' which consists in removing the pavement and blocks from the bed of the sluice, gathering the precious compost, and replacing or renewing the blocks and stones of the pavement—severely punished by the violence of rock and water.

One would suppose that these 'cleaning-up-times' were seasons of excitement, resembling the drawing of a lottery; but this is not so. When the average of the gravel has once been ascertained, expert miners will calculate almost to a nicety the amount, monthly or bi-monthly, of their gross profits. The last step of the process is the retorting of the amalgam. Under a fierce heat, the evaporated quicksilver is collected and preserved for further use; whilst the royal metal—after the fashion of martyrs—emerges from prolonged torment, perfect and pure.

Where the *cañon* narrowed to a cleft we halted and retraced our steps; and then climbed a lofty gravel isthmus, dividing this first hollow from another and deeper ravine, in which a second 'monitor' was in position. By this time, the cough had fairly mastered me; and I was fain to sit down and rest whilst the others went on their way. I may thank that enforced pause for a very curious effect.

After brief breathing space, I strolled to and fro over the vast mound—the isthmus on one side widened into a plateau—collecting handfuls of gravel at random, with a purpose that will be made plain hereafter: having obtained a sufficiency of these, I sat down near the verge of the cliff, which, at this point, fell some two hundred feet sheer. As I rested there, my thoughts travelled away over many leagues of land and sea—perhaps, I had begun to drowse, as one is apt to do when weak and weary: at any rate, the dream was broken somewhat startlingly. Right under my feet came that savage hiss and roar; and the earth literally and palpably trembled—not with comparatively slow undulation, as in the Franciscan quake, but with a rapid quiver as of mortal fear. The instantaneous transition from complete repose to the extreme of insecurity was very remarkable; resembling the sensations of an evil dream where, without previous warning, you find yourself sliding over the marge of a precipice—both foot and handhold failing. For a second or two, it seemed as if the face of the cliff must needs topple outwards and downwards incontinently, bearing me along with it; and I cannot deny having retreated inland somewhat hastily, before I realised the cause of the phenomenon.

Nothing could be simpler after all. The monitor below—held in abeyance like its fellow for the same reason—had, without note of preparation, opened fire. This once understood, I became much comforted and encouraged; and advanced cautiously—keeping a little wide of the presumed line of battery—till, lying prone, I could peer over the verge of the cliff. Of the face of the breach nothing could be seen; for not only did the bank sheer rather inwards here, but a dense mist of dust and spray spread far around the point of impact; however, in the little group, from the centre of which shot forth the level streak of grey, I made out the Sailor directing the monitor. I doubt if the heaviest piece of ordnance served by the Naval Brigade ever wrought, within the same space, such havoc as the harmless-looking engine then a-plying. Some hundreds of tons of displaced rock and gravel witnessed, I was told, to the luck, or accuracy, of our comrade's aim.

When the rest of the party rejoined me, the purpose of our visit was nearly fulfilled; but, before climbing the track leading back to the manager's hut, we halted by the side of a rill, to make experiment of the gravel-samples I had collected, and of others selected likewise at random, not only from the surface, but from such depths as a spade could reach easily.

This panning — still in vogue amongst the 'streamers' of the Cornish moors—is the rudest of all mining processes, and quite infantile in its simplicity. In a broad shallow vessel—an ordinary shovel will suffice at a pinch—you sift a few handfuls of gravel to and fro; gradually casting out the refuse, and adding fresh water till there is left a *residuum* scarcely coarser than sand: in this you must look for 'colour'—the miner's term for presence of gold.

Ours might possibly have been the proverbial luck of *les mains vierges;* but in no one instance were our pains fruitless. At the bottom of each pan, without exception, glistened, more or less frequently, the soft yellow specks, minishing from scales like flattened pin-heads, to grains almost invisible. This does not sound very grand, perhaps; but if you remember that these were only samples, culled from the surface of a mass, estimated to contain millions upon millions of tons; and that the material invariably waxes greatly richer as the 'bed-rock' is neared, the result will not seem contemptible. We, at least, were more than satisfied; and, albeit frequent disappointments had made some amongst us slow to admire, none would have inscribed this forenoon amongst the wasted days.

After doing justice to the miner's good fare, we followed a rough team-road, a league farther into the hills into another valley, where an adit-level, or tunnel, has been driven in upon the bed-rock itself; whence is extracted 'cement,' so hard and tough as only to be worked in a steam-mill. It is, of course, proportionably more valuable—averaging, as we were informed, about eight dollars per ton; whereas about twenty cents in the blue gravel, and eight cents in the grey upper strata, seems a fair average.

Here you may actually walk on the floor of the 'dead river' and touch stones, rounded by a current that must have ceased to flow, Science says, ages before there is record of man's existence. To a technical eye the sight must be rarely attractive, and I shall not easily forget our Professor's face, as he issued from those darkling recesses; through grime and moisture it beamed with geological ecstasy.

We reached Nevada long after sundown, but just in time for supper; and fell-to with a pleasant consciousness that it had been fairly earned. On the morrow we returned to Colfax by different routes, for reasons good.

The one selected by the Sailor and myself abounded in steep and 'soft' places; but was incomparably the most picturesque I have traversed in Western America. It would be difficult to conceive richer variety of mountain, wood and water; and, as a final *tableau*, right over against you as you near Colfax, looms grand Cape Horn, dipping its feet into a turbid river.

Before closing this chapter, I should like to sum up briefly the observations already recorded: the subject is surely of sufficient importance to warrant this.

The advantages of hydraulic mines seem to be—the absolute certainty and uniformity of profits, inasmuch as any variation must needs be on a steady ascending scale—their great durability, and comparative immunity against accident—the marvellous cheapness of the process, after the preliminary expenses of reservoirs, flumes, and tunnels have once been cleared.

The first of these assertions will scarcely be doubted by those who can comprehend that, by sinking of shafts at intervals, the extent of the 'Lead,' or auriferous bed, can be staked out to a few fathoms; and that the increasing value of the gravel, as it nears the 'bed-rock,' is a fact established by universal experience.

The second is not less easily demonstrable. The material to be dealt with, lies, so to speak, patent—more easy and certain of mensuration than even a coal-field, or any other known mineral reserve; no costly and perishable machinery, such as mills, engines, pumps, or hoisting gear, are in use; whilst the inclemency of seasons is likely rather to aid, than impede, progress. When the heaven is black with clouds, and there is threat of great rain, the gold seeker's heart leaps with joy; and of snow he knows little or nothing, save when brimming reservoirs, and flumes lip-full, tell of drifts melting in the higher Sierras.

As to the third—I believe the table of comparative cost, given above, to be absolutely beyond question. Setting adits and tunnels aside, even pick and shovel are rarely required; and no 'plant' is in use that cannot be constructed and repaired by any intelligent smith or carpenter. The consistency of the gravel or cement, varies, and it should always be remembered that the richest is the most impracticable; but, taking a fair average, it may be estimated that a supply of three hundred water inches will enable two men to displace about three thousand tons in a day of twelve hours. And these need not be athletes either, judging from the specimens serving that first monitor. I gravely doubt if, in any other mining district, that crabbed, crook-backed elder would have been deemed worth his hire. A few hands are employed, watching the flumes and keeping the sluice-ways clear; but this is essentially cheap labour, and specially suited to the feeble Chinese folk, to whom it is often assigned. On 'cleaning-up' days, the manager usually dispenses with heathen company; not caring to trust those long finger-nails too near the soft amalgam. So—put working expenses at ten, or even twelve cents, and the gross value at fifteen cents per ton of displaced material—the daily return will not be unsatisfactory for operations conducted on so small a scale. As a rule, it may be reckoned that profits rise more than in proportion to the increase of water power.

On the debit side must be set down the preliminary and precautionary expenses—in some cases very heavy. In one instance, over a million dollars have been sunk without a dividend in sight, and without a murmur from those chiefly interested; and this property—controlled by some of the cleverest capitalists in California—will, doubtless, eventually more than pay its way. The blasting adits are only needed to burst, so to speak, the last barriers of the treasure-house, when the 'bed-rock' is near; but, except in localities exceptionally favoured—where a natural cleft or *cañon* serves the same purpose—a tunnel to carry off the outflow is obviously necessary. If you consider that this may have to be driven inch by inch, by dint of drill, through granite, quartz, or volcanic formations almost as hard, it is easy to imagine the cost and labour involved. Furthermore, as we said above, the immunity from accidents is comparative. Flumes are liable to leakage, and reservoir-dams to burst; and, though the first is trivial and easily amended, the last is a grave disaster. For, not only is the repairing of the embankment, with its massive bracings and buttresses of hewn timber, very costly, but much precious working time may be lost before the water-reserves are again available. However, some kind of risk is, I presume, inseparable from any venture, whether by land or sea; and the risks here seem about as light as are consistent with fair mercantile speculation.

Finally, though, when certain *data* are established, a progression of profits is almost assured, the ascending scale is minutely graduated; and there is a moderation about the whole concern.

Property of this kind, worked as is described above, may pay good dividends for a couple of generations; waxing richer as the core of the treasure is approached—but slowly—never electrifying its shareholders with a brilliant discovery, or stunning them by a dismal disaster. On the whole, it appears a field rather for investment than speculation.

One word more, before quitting the subject. Since seeing the high rates of interest prevalent out here, and the numberless enterprises in which money can be turned over rapidly, I do not lay so much stress on the argument, that, if an American property be really valuable, it will never pass out of American hands. However, if this theory be at all reliable, it needs must bear a double edge.

Now, since the mines of Nevada County have been in full work, they have been supported almost entirely by Californian capital. Only a very few, quite recently—and these, as I am informed, not the choicest, albeit fair, specimens of their class—have been 'promoted' beyond the Atlantic. For example, the property we inspected has been worked for a dozen years or more by native proprietors; its name is neither of good nor evil repute in the British mining market; nor, so far as I know, is it likely to become famous or infamous there. Nevertheless, to avoid possible cause of offence, I have purposely abstained from more than vaguely indicating the *locale.*

Possibly some of my readers may think it worth while to work out for themselves, in detail, these rough outlines. Simply as a spectacle, the scene I have tried to describe amply repays a visit. To see the hand of Nature turned literally against herself, with such terrible effect, rather raises one's conceptions of the supremacy of Man.

CHAPTER XII.

Now that we are back on the frontier, it is time to take up a theme recently alluded to, which engrossed many of my thoughts whilst sojourning in San Francisco.

I but impute to others a negligence to which I must personally plead guilty, in assuming that only her metalliferous resources have made California familiar to English ears. Plain, uncommercial people, who never open the *Mark Lane Express*, or care for the fluctuations of markets, might be surprised to hear that the above-mentioned source of revenue may eventually prove not the richest allotted to this favoured State. I say—not the richest; because certainty, and durability, must count largely in the intrinsic value of any possession whatsoever.

None will deny, and many have heavy reasons for affirming, that from any search after the nobler metals some insecurity is inseparable: perhaps, were it otherwise, these ventures might lose somewhat of their fascination. Even the auriferous gravels, whereof we have just been speaking, though they may outlast a generation beyond our own, must in process of time disappear; and though the treasures of granite and limestone already open may stand an amount of drain quite incalculable, and be supplemented by yet vaster discoveries, it is possible that these may minish, if not fail; whilst to each successive enterprise must attach the like element of hazard. These are considerations rather for posterity, and may concern little you who read, or me who write; but to the historical future of a great country they may be of grave import.

Certain words are writ in a Book true to a letter, though we may often misinterpret its meaning: they were uttered six thousand years ago, near an altar built in the shadow of Ararat, on ground scarce dried from the Deluge; and thus they run,—*While the earth remaineth, seed time and harvest, and cold and heat, and summer and winter, and day and night shall not cease.*

Since that gracious benison was laid on her, rarely has the Great Mother shown herself more bounteous than on the plains stretching from the Sierras to the Pacific. There are table-lands, nooks, and valleys, far up amongst the hill-spurs, naturally perhaps more fertile than the low-lying country watered by the San Joaquin and Sacramento rivers; but these have, thus far, been only partially broken up; and from the latter chiefly are drawn supplies of wheat so vast, that this item of export alone would insure to any country commercial importance.

Striking a rough balance from the official returns of the last seven years, about four million sacks, of one hundred pounds each, seem to have been shipped annually; and last harvest—an unusually productive one—would raise the average considerably.* This is in the face of a largely increased home-consumption, and prices generally ruling high. The Chilian and Australian varieties seem to suit the soil best; and the grain, though hard and difficult to grind, is plump in ear and exceptionally rich in gluten.

The dangerous facilities of agriculture here have been already alluded to; dangerous—because the husbandman, waxing over-confident, if not supine, may forget to provide against the losses that two successive seasons of drought must needs entail.

* Vide Appendix D. (1).

The early sown crops, though ultimately less productive, suffer least from a partial rain failure; but the risk always exists, and must endure till a complete and uniform system of irrigation is established.

About this there need be no doubt or real difficulty.* The natural conformation of the country is, in most places, specially favourable to such projects; and the water stored up in mountain tarns, or running to waste from the foot-hills, to say nothing of the abundant rivers, would more than suffice all possible demands. I met in San Francisco an eminent engineer, who has devoted himself specially to this branch of his profession, and had lately returned from superintending similar undertakings on a very large scale in the Deccan. He assured me that the obstacles to be overcome might be compassed by any ordinary contractor; and instanced one case, where a large district might be thoroughly protected by a simple canal, at a comparatively small cost. His figures are unluckily mislaid; but I am sure that if the expense had been fairly assessed, about a dollar per acre would have covered it; and by such insurance against the caprice of seasons, the value of the land would be quite doubled.

* Vide Appendix D. (2).

In many parts of the State barley thrives wonderfully well, and produces most of the 'volunteer crops.' These spring simply from the grain shaken out in harvesting; and, very often, the seed is worked in only by harrowing, without use of the plough. Sonoma County, stretching to the north-west of the San Pablo Bay, is famous for maize; but its culture does not seem so much affected here as in Iowa and Illinois.

The danger of drought once overpast, the crop, whether in ear or swathe, is safe from the wrath of the elements: neither is there much to fear from such minor plagues as blight or wire-worm. Yet, till his produce is fairly on shipboard, the Californian farmer can scarce sit down to count his gains. When the ripening process has once begun, it progresses very rapidly, and with wonderful uniformity throughout each district; thereby involving a proportionate demand for labour. Over a million acres are at the present time under wheat; and I am personally acquainted with the owner of a *rancho* in the San Joaquin Valley, where six thousand acres in a ring-fence are so cultivated.* If the crop be reaped a week too soon, it will naturally sample

* Vide Appendix D. (3).

badly, and be apt to spoil; if a week too late—the husk being parched—there will be cruel waste in the gathering. At such an anxious season, it is not hard to fancy what manner of prayer a pious husbandman would address to the Lord of the Harvest.

Scarcely second in importance to her cereals, is the wool produce of California. The exports of this commodity in 1855 were under four hundred thousand pounds. In 1871 it approached eleven thousand tons, at a largely increased value. You may remember the story of the Scotch noble, who after exhibiting to Prince Esterhazy his flocks, then unparalleled in the country for numbers and quality, inquired how many sheep his visitor owned. Answered the calm Magyar—"I cannot tell; but I own a few thousand shepherds." Some of the great *rancheros* of Southern California would be fain to speak almost as vaguely: therefore our numerical calculations must be somewhat rough. After careful inquiry, and some study of these statistics, I am inclined to believe that the annual clip exceeds three million fleeces; whilst tens of thousands of sheep, from disease, wide straying, and other causes, never come under the shears. Neither cost nor pains have been spared to procure judicious crosses; an the texture of the wool, originally very coarse and fibrous, has been infinitely improved of late, though it cannot as yet hold its own with Europe or Australia.

A dry season tells, naturally, on the pasturage, no less than on the tilths; but, on these occasions, superior quality often goes far to make amends for the gross deficiency. In like manner, the sheep-farmer of the northern counties—breeding entirely from imported rams, or crosses direct from the Eastern States—though his flocks never multiply like those browsing southwards of Lake Tularé, almost balances the account on the higher value of his sample.

One might, no doubt, find parallels, without going further afield than our Scottish Highlands: indeed, I question if any single Californian owns possessions vast as the appanages of Sutherland, Athol, or Breadalbane.* Nevertheless, there is a fine flavour of suzerainty about these noble southern *ranchos;* specially when you remember that they are made up, not of bleak hills and desolate corries, fit only for the harbour of deer and browsing of hardy hill-sheep, but of pasture sweet as ever fatted kine, and of loam rich as was ever turned by ploughshare. Sixteen square miles was no

* Vide Appendix D. (4).

uncommon area for one of the old 'Spanish grants,' most of which have now passed in their entirety out of Mexican into American hands. I was presented to a veteran general officer of the U. S. A.—like a picture by Vandyck, with his pointed white beard and clear-cut features—who owned two hundred thousand acres down in fair Los Angeles. Not the lightest of many like vexations, was my regret in being forced to decline his hospitality. For one, who was his guest last autumn, had told me of the abundance of game, great and small, in those parts, and of the facilities of pursuit; and on question of *venerie* it is tolerably safe to trust a scion of the M'Callum More. It seems, as if a slight parody on the old hunting-ditty might serve here

What shall be our sport to-day?
Shall it be deer or bear?
There's nothing too long, too fast, too gay
For me and the good bay mare.

Fancy a 'grizzly' lassoed fairly in the open. Surely, rarer sport has not often been seen since, in the Great Circus, men looked down on the feats of the *bestiarii*.

The world runs all in cycles, they say; therefore it is, perhaps, that in some of these recent settlements you find reproduced, so exactly, some of the most ancient phases of Eastern life. In the count, however, of his flocks and herds the Western patriarch far outruns his antitype. About a year ago, one of the old Spanish colonists dwelling in San Diego, for reasons best known to his solemn self, wishing to migrate, offered to take one dollar per head for his live stock of every sort and kind, and throw in the fee simple of the land. An Eastern speculator—from Chicago, if I remember right—came to trade; but returned, *re infectâ*, simply because his capital caved in, long before the numbering of the droves was done.

When the Sacramento river ran through a swampy desert, and never a sail had been furled within the Golden Gates, all down the seaboard, from Monterey to the southernmost boundary of Los Angeles, were found, neither few nor far between, snug home-farms, fertile and carefully tended as husbandman could desire. Here dwelt the old Mission fathers in great comfort, and perhaps not a little indolence; for their preacher-work was easy, and the mild Indian converts did all the labour needful in the facile soil. Amongst many good legacies bequeathed by these honest Padres to ungrateful successors, not the least precious are myriads of well-nurtured vines. One of these, twining round the mouldering walls of a deserted Mission in Santa Barbara, has long been a miracle of fruitfulness and luxuriance ; and shows no sign of decay, though near a century has passed since it was severed from the parent-stem in Catalonia.

Now-a-days, vineyards have sprung up in almost every part of the State. Indeed, the Lower Sierras, and the valleys trending coastwards from the foot-hills, produce liquor more palateable than that pressed from the 'Mission' grape ; for the excess of saccharine in the latter makes the wine somewhat heavy and cloying : so the trade of Sonoma, Napa, and El Dorado—all lying north of the Golden Gates—has already surpassed that of the southern counties whence it was derived. Of late years, cuttings from some of the most famous stocks of Burgundy, Gascony, and the Rhineland have been planted with very promising results ; and infinitely more care and skill have been bestowed on the process of fermentation and refining : until recently, these had been conducted much on the principle of the First husbandman. The total annual produce has risen to ten millions of gallons, and is still steadily on the increase; whilst the wines average a better price than most *ordinaires:* so that they must please a goodly number of palates, albeit to an old-fashioned taste the finest seem not devoid of a certain roughness and crudity.

From time primeval, the olive and the vine have thriven side by side; and Southern California is no exception to the rule. The groves encompassing each and every one of the old Missions have been utilised and much amplified of late; and Santa Barbara alone sends forth annually a hundred thousand gallons or so of oil, scarcely inferior to any that flows from Italian or Spanish presses. In truth, the bounteous soil of these counties welcomes kindly almost every known fruit-bearing tree. Specially do the fig and orange flourish here. The latter has been sedulously cultivated, with no small profit; for, when nine seasons have brought it to maturity, each tolerably prolific orange-tree is worth some twenty dollars annually.*

The agreeable little hand-book, referred to above, notices the extensive planting of mulberries to supply food to the silkworm; for sericulture has become a Californian industry. But on this sub-

* Vide Appendix D. (5).

ject I can speak neither from personal knowledge nor accurate information: therefore I simply *guarda è passa.*

In filling the last dozen pages with dry details, my chief object has been to prove to whoso it may concern, that the promises, wherewith California tempts persons about to emigrate, in no wise resemble the prospectus of the ingenious Mr. Scadder. Perhaps the most substantial advantage lies in the great variety of soil and climate. Any practical farmer—taking due care that his lines fall aright—could not fail in finding work at once ready to his hand. Indeed, in some of those southern districts, I imagine capital, sagely invested, might bring in liberal returns, when backed by no great skill or experience.

In such a region, even our sanguine friend, Captain Longsword, who seems to think that the purchase system, just abolished in the service, survives in agriculture—so that, by risk of his modest savings, he can at once be invested with a fresh commission bearing Queen Ceres' sign-manual—might sit down here in comparative safety under his own fig-tree. For, when once fairly established, ordinary gardening skill will keep a vineyard in order; whilst an orange grove needs no more tending than an orchard; and our 'plunger,' when on leave, had ever a hankering for horticulture, and a happy knack of wielding the pruning-knife.

Furthermore, though there is doubtless room, and to spare, for large investors, I conceive that very modest capital can nowhere else be worked to more advantage. Take an instance, unluckily by no means rare.

Many of us know—and, not being his tormented landlord, perhaps compassionate—Jacob Moldwarp. He was hale and hearty enough when, in early married days, he ventured on Hungerford Farm, poor land at the best, and soured from stint of manure. The first wet spring threw him behindhand; and, floundering on doggedly ever since, he has never got quite clear of the slough. So far from putting money aside to start them in life, he can scarce find bread and bacon enough for his big growing family: each rent-day, as he shambles in half sullen, half ashamed, with the same stale excuses, deepens the lines on his gaunt face, and the shifty look in his eyes, till he appears like a fraudulent bankrupt rather than a 'right down British yeoman.' Yet it is not so. Jacob would cheat no one willingly of his due—not even his landlord; but the old burden, want of capital, under which stronger shoulders have bowed themselves, has broken him down.

Now set this man and his belongings down in the San Joaquin Valley, and see how they would fare. Land—provided it were tolerably remote from Stockton—he might purchase at thirty shillings per acre; frame-house, cattle-sheds, and a light barn or so, supposing the ground bare of such conveniences, could be set up in a few days; and the surplus that would probably result from the sale of the live and dead stock on Hungerford Farm would more than plenish the new homestead. And those long-limbed lads and sturdy 'mawthers,' who at the home rate of wages were scarce worth their salt—at what would you appraise them in a country where reliable labour is eagerly secured at two dollars a day and upwards, and at certain seasons is almost priceless? Moreover, suppose him enabled to grow four successive wheat crops on the same ground, without fear of permanently impoverishing it, much less of being called to account for breaking the course. After a season or two at this work, specially if no heavy drought intervene, I doubt if his bitterest enemy—his late landlord's agent, to wit—would know Jacob Moldwarp again.

The climate of the interior, where the sea breezes may not penetrate, is, no doubt, at first rather trying. To dwell from May to December under a sky rainless, cloudless, windless, must ever be a cross to the Teuton or Anglo-Saxon, though a Provençal or Calabrian would be little like to grumble. But, so far as I can learn, this regular drought brings no inevitable disease in its train; and the country, as a rule, is singularly free from epidemics. An unusual dry spring, may lengthen the bills of mortality no less than other debits; and even the vine-growers, whose profits are largely increased thereby, would be moved to deprecate such a season. On the whole, however, foreigners seem to become easily and quickly acclimatised.

Lastly, as to the price of land.

There is room enough for all, and more than all, that are like to come hither; for, out of forty million acres in this State fit for tillage, scarce a thirtieth part has been touched by plough or spade. Nevertheless, estates are no longer to be had for a 'song'—not even such a costly one as La

Diva trills. In certain districts, lots of a hundred and sixty acres can still be taken up at the government price of a dollar and a quarter ; but these, as a rule, are too remote, or otherwise undesirable, to tempt ordinary emigrants. Vast tracts have been granted to railroads already laid, or in process of construction ; and real property has become, of late, rather a favourite speculation with the native capitalists. Moreover, it would be hard to set forth a regular tariff; for the value of land, even in the same county, would vary considerably, according to its proximity to rail or river. The transport of his produce must for years to come enter largely into a Californian farmer's calculation.

In the Sacramento and San Joaquin Valleys—excluding property in near vicinage to the larger towns—from five to fifteen dollars might be a fair average; in Sonoma, Napa, and Solano it is slightly higher. In San Mateo, which the wealthy Franciscan chiefly affects for his *villeggiatura*, ground commands a fancy price; but the average falls again greatly as you travel southward, so that in Santa Barbara, San Diego, and San Bernardino, choice *ranchos* are to be secured at from two to three dollars per acre.

Especially, however, in these southern counties

does it behove a purchaser to look narrowly into his title. With the 'Spanish grants' there has already been endless trouble. Doubtless in almost all instances the languid, credulous Mexican got much the worse of the 'trade' with the keen American lawyer or mortgagee; but the Don's descendants have, to a certain extent, avenged him by involving these properties in a perfect mist of litigation. This has been almost entirely swept away by the strong patience of the law; but it is still needful, before signing and sealing, to take all possible precautions. 'Black mailing' is not entirely confined to the mines.

These calculations, remember, are based absolutely on the present state of things. A few years, or even a few months, might work material changes. Two important lines of rail, now actually in progress, the Atlantic and Pacific starting from St. Louis—the Southern Pacific with Memphis for its eastern terminus—will cross and recross these same southern counties; and, as the supply of their special produce can scarcely ever equal the demand, it is not difficult to foresee how the real property market here will be affected by unlimited facilities of transport.*

Surely, it might be well worth the while of

* Vide Appendix D. (6).

anyone, well versed in the emigration question, to take stock in earnest of this country's capabilities. In some of the districts named above, where British settlers are almost unknown, I verily believe limited capital and limited experience would meet with better, because more varied, opportunities of profitable development than in Illinois, Iowa, or even the Southern Dominion. And, for the benefit of any who may be moved to judge for themselves whether these sketches have been over-coloured, I would alter slightly a well-worn proverb, and say—'The more haste, the better speed.'*

* Vide Appendix D. (7).

CHAPTER XIII.

We paused, or turned aside, no more on our way back to Salt Lake City. The clemency of the weather, though it was not yet quite settled, enabled us to appreciate several points of view scarcely noticed before. Pleasant Valley has earned its name; and the *cañon* of the Palisades, where sheer cliff walls, penning in the Humboldt, almost baffle the sunlight, makes a good sombre picture—especially in the easternmost gorge, where the stream, chafed with long struggle for freedom, rushes on for a while with the impulse and puissance of a real mountain river. So, over alkali plains, leaden marsh flats, and dusky sage-brush, around the head of the Great Lake to the Mormon city once more; where—in default of other entertainment—we were refreshed with home news, after more than a three weeks' fast.

Out of the four days of our stay, we gave one entirely to Camp Douglas. Setting aside pleasant recollections of the place, we wished to observe minutely the daily routine and economy of the service; and the courtesy of our hosts enabled us to do this thoroughly. The details would probably rather weary, than interest, general readers; but, on the whole, we were much pleased with what we saw. In point of scrupulous neatness the barrack-rooms would compare unfavourably with ours; and I doubt if an inspection of 'necessaries' would satisfy a martinet: but the accommodation—to say nothing of the officers' quarters—is more spacious, the rations more liberal, and altogether there seems to be more consideration for the comfort of the full private than our military rulers have yet cared to bestow.

Before evening parade, we had some practice with the Gatling mitrailleuse. It seemed, both to the Sailor and myself, lighter and more manageable than any European model; whilst its accuracy at a certain range, and rapidity of sweep, were marvellous. I have looked on many engines of war more potent in outward seeming, but on a more venomous never; and the whole effect was produced by turning a handle with something less than the ordinary energy of an organ-grinder. But, I think, the streets in which this instrument shall be plied, will find it something more than a 'nuisance;' and in the concerts in which it takes part there will be no great struggle for front places.

When evening parade was nearly over, we walked round to where, some thirty paces in rear of the supernumerary rank, were ranged the Mormon prisoners, then awaiting their trial on charges somewhat similar to those on which their President had been arraigned.

A douce homely folk they seemed on the whole; and even the expression of the 'Hickman' aforesaid—hired assassin and highway robber by his own confession—was rather cunning than malign. But almost every visage wore the same sly, shifty look. Not being well read in the Mormon creed, I cannot say whether its devotees are expressly forbidden to gaze straight and steadfastly into the face of either friend or foe.

The fourth morning found us journeying eastwards again; and, mounting in daylight the Wahsatch passes, which we had descended darkling, we were fain to allow that they did redeem much of the monotony of the rest of the route betwixt Ogden and Omaha. In the *cañons* of Weber and Echo, there is no lack of rugged grandeur; nor of a softer beauty amongst the coils of the Green River; and divers *buttes*, near the Point of Rocks, are so fantastically carven, that it would seem as if some old-world architect had chosen this for a practice-ground. The clear sky began to lower ominously as we grated through the drift-cuttings, still deep and solid, of the Laramie Plains; and we fancied that our engineers made better speed, as though conscious of the burden of the atmosphere and the wrath to come: if so, truly they were wise; for heavy white flakes were driving densely as we crossed the Sherman ridge, and the track—closing in behind us—was blocked for three full days ensuing. But at Cheyenne we could afford to mock at the Erl King; and, in the forenoon of the morrow, Omaha was made actually 'on time.'

Here, we found the same intelligent official who at Laramie had sent us on our way unrejoicing. To his good nature we were indebted for the better view of the new Missouri bridge than could otherwise have been obtained; for the curves of the approach are so abrupt that, even standing on the platform of the car, you see little or nothing till the portal-tower is passed. But from the driving engine, where we were perched, the effect is very striking. For nearly half a mile the roadway hangs in mid-air at such a height that the welter against the piers of the turbid current can scarcely be discerned; and an ordinary traffic steamer, anchored hard by, looked scarcely larger than a Thames 'Citizen.' Indeed the whole structure is a triumph of Western engineering and iron foundry; for the embankments are laid across a kind of morass; and many fathoms of treacherous mud and shifting soil must have been pierced before the supports found firm foothold in the Missouri. If, as we were assured, no pains have been spared to make the work solid and secure to the minutest detail—and the small vibration on the bridge, added to the smoothness of a track partly laid within that same week, would go far to prove this—it is the more creditable that the original estimate should have exceeded the actual cost by some thousands of dollars.

Thenceforward to Chicago, the way was plain and absolutely uninteresting.

Here we tarried only long enough to shift our belongings into the sleeping-car of the eastward-bound train; for here the 'Arlington' and her freight were bound to part, with regrets, I hope, not all one-sided. Not being in her first youth, she was apt to give in her joints, and wax creaky at times, the good old car; and, whilst in her convoy, all of us had known some weariness—some not a little pain, nevertheless, on the whole, we had had a right good time; and nowhere else, of a surety, could we have fared half so merrily. A dash of the ludicrous, unluckily, often attaches itself to African emotions; yet, I think, no Britisher was much moved to laughter, when the round rolling eyes of our chief henchman moistened visibly as he bade us farewell.

We are never like again to foregather. But may luck wait on the ready wit and nimble hands of our zealous Conductor; blessings on the curly pow of Andrew, simply smiling; and may the unctuous countenance of Joe of the caboose shine still with the oil of gladness above his fellows!

For thirty hours ensuing we sped smoothly on along the southern shore of Lake Erie to Buffalo and thence to Albany—the day breaking just in time to reveal the chief beauties of the Hudson above the Palisades. It chances that I have looked on this noble river only

> In the first of the morning twilight,
> When the trees are merely grey.

Nevertheless, in my memory it has no rival. Certain points of view do assuredly remind one of the Upper Meuse; but the Hudson boasts far richer expanse and variety of woodland, infinitely grander cliffs, and a volume of water beyond compare. The Sailor and Tressilian, viewing it for the first time, were, I fancy, more impressed by this spectacle than by any other American wonder. Despite of 'improvements,' Nature still queens it here; nor can the villas and the country houses, dotted about so densely, entirely mar the landscape; indeed, certain coigns of vantage—few and far between, of course—seem hardly changed since stout Hendrick rounded them in his galliot.

At the New York Terminus, the small company, which for so long had made up a not inharmonious unity, was resolved into its several elements; and I am fain to believe that in the farewell cocktail compounded by our Commodore, there mingled no drop bitterer than the juice of Angostura.

CHAPTER XIV.

Shortly before our arrival a truce had been sounded in Wall Street, after a contest fierce and prolonged, waged on the old Erie battle-ground. Sharp skirmishing for some time past had brought on a general engagement, in which the bears—fairly 'cornered' at last—had been defeated with great loss. And now the victors were dividing the spoil, sometimes not over amicably; and the vanquished, who had not sought safer hiding places, were binding up their wounds in their tents. For from such a fight many must needs come out sorely stricken—some so sorely, that if they would carry on the war, they will be fain, instead of caracolling gaily in the van, to join Sydney Smith's 'heavy brigade of bankrupts, with *mourir sans payer* on their banners, and *Aere alieno* on their trumpets.' And the dead? Well—in this enterprising community, even social annihilalation is very rare; and over commercial tombs that seemed securely closed, might usually be written an ignoble *Resurgam.*

That same afternoon, in the pleasant morning room of the Union Club, I was saluted by a member with whom I had been made slightly acquainted during our previous sojourn here. He was a man of mark in more ways than one; for his bold operations, backed by solid capital, had made the Erie Ring to quake in the zenith of their power; and, unless their hide was taunt-proof, they must often have winced under his bitter tongue.

After interchange of greeting and enquiries, this eminent person proceeded :—

"You missed a good deal last week. Even a look-in in Wall Street was worth something. It was warm down there, I tell you."

Freedom of interrogation grows upon one in this great country. Therefore I ventured to ask, whilst partaking of a fragrant mint julep at his cost, how my entertainer himself had fared in that conflict—not, I own, expecting a very direct reply. He answered promptly, and, as it seemed, quite frankly:

"I wasn't right in the swim—went in on

Tuesday morning, and cleared out by Friday noon —but I bested 'em for about half-a-million."

Evincing, I hope, all outward and visible signs of implicit faith, I was troubled with misgivings lest this famous *farceur* had been practising on British credulity. But one who bore him no good-will, more than confirmed this statement—on oath too, so to speak—an hour later; so that I was fain to accept it as quasi-historical.

But transatlantic figures—insist as much as you will on the difference between dollars and pounds sterling—will, to the end, rather stagger and confuse European arithmetic. Certainly, the more you hear of such matters, the less you wonder at the lavish expense and luxury prevalent here. After all, it is only the old Homburg life over again on a larger scale. Would the digestion, even of moderate punters, then, have been impaired by a rise of thirty kreutzers in the *foies de volaille à la brochette*; or if Conrad (with whom be peace!) had arbitrarily doubled the tariff, would the '*Piper sec*' have slaked the thirst of victors or vanquished less gratefully? I trow not. You may find heavy gamblers, both with scrip and pasteboard, thrifty to the hoarding of a cheese-paring; but I question if these exceptions will much weaken the rule of recklessness.

Whilst speaking on such topics, one's thoughts naturally revert to a personage, famous on both sides of the Atlantic; the very whisper of whose name makes the ears of Wall Street to tingle—I mean, of course, *the* Vanderbilt.

The next day, driving back through Central Park—we were trying a famous team, and had gone out early, so as to 'speed' them when the Lane was comparatively clear—we met a wagon, drawn by a pair of raking browns, going at the lazy loping gait noticeable in many trotting celebrities when not extended. In the shadow of the hood sat a tall, spare, erect, old man; severe and somewhat stately of aspect; with a touch of the precisian in the trim of his beard, the fashion of his sombre apparel, and the turn of his broad-brimmed beaver. Neither in figure nor feature was there the faintest resemblance; yet something in his *pose* and method of handling the reins, reminded me at once of a deceased dignitary, better known in the Row than in Convocation; though austere dignity was assuredly not a leading characteristic of the Dean of St. Buryans. In acknowledgment of my companion's cheery hail, this solemn elder vouchsafed a short surly nod, but scarcely a side glance out of his hard steady eyes; and yet the two had been intimate for years, and not seldom had made venture in the same argosy. That afternoon I heard, in order and detail, a story of which I had gotten only a disjointed outline; though, it is needless to say, no business secrets were betrayed.

There is neither mystery nor obscurity about Vanderbilt's early career. He began life as a 'long shore boatman or pilot, and was afterwards promoted to command one of the innumerable steamers running to and fro in the Bay and Sound. Mere thrift could scarcely have laid even the first foundation stone of his fortune. It is said that some of his regular passengers, authorities in Wall Street, supplied him with information, and allowed him to stand in occasionally; and—once having 'bank money' in hand—he backed the run dauntlessly. But the inconceivably rapid progress by which competence was converted into wealth, has never been satisfactorily explained; as for gaining information from the man himself—it were as well to seek it from an ancient grave. His name was hardly known on Change before it became a power there; and, very soon afterwards, he took the chief place in the Board-room of the Company whose boats he had steered. Hence, I believe, rather than from his connection with any regular yacht squadron, he derives his brevet of Commodore. No amount of audacity or astuteness, unsupported by strong capital, would have enabled him to carry out the gigantic schemes of aggrandisement, scarce one of which seems to have gone awry. Of these a single example—the most famous of all, and comparatively recent—may suffice.

Almost from its commencement, Vanderbilt had been largely interested in the New York Central Railroad; and, as the shares fluctuated considerably for a while, watching the market warily, he was enabled to acquire almost absolute control of the line. Two or three directors followed his lead implicitly; whilst the rest soon found that it was useless to struggle against the Commodore and his host of proxies. In truth, none had reason to grumble. The line was admirably managed and well supported —paying, despite large outlay on depôts, store houses, and rolling stock, very satisfactory dividends; and though Vanderbilt, while his plans were maturing, overtly meddled little with the stock, the shares rose steadily.

One Saturday evening, two hours before midnight, such directors as could be found in New York, were convened to an 'urgent special meeting.' My informant sat on that memorable board; and described very quaintly the fear and quaking with which he and others, albeit used to their chief's strategy then listened to the propounding of his sovereign will. The Commodore was pleased to argue—or rather to insist—that the value of all improvements and augmentations, effected since the commencement of the line, should be considered as so much surplus capital; and, on these grounds, proposed to declare a dividend of eighty per cent. on the original shares. There was much surprise, no doubt; and probably some strong language accompanied weak resistance; but, for the reasons stated above, before the chairman had finished speaking, the question was virtually carried.

If the minds of so well-trained an audience were perturbed, what, think you, was the effect out of doors on the morrow, when the announcement of the Vanderbilt *coup* spread abroad like wildfire? Probably, never since its institution did a Sabbath more thoroughly belie its name. From early morning till long past midnight, the saloons and corridors of the Fifth Avenue Hotel—then, as now, a kind of supplementary Stock Exchange—were thronged with haggard, anxious faces, and filled with an uproar of eager voices, wherein the Yankee twang, the Southern drawl, and the Semitic snuffle struggled for mastery. Yet this scene was tranquil compared to that enacted in Wall Street, on the Monday forenoon. The place was verily and literally a 'bear-garden;' and the author of all this turmoil sat chuckling grimly—not more, perhaps, over his financial triumphs, than over a consciousness that even his nearest familiars had been taken thoroughly unawares. On none did the *coup* light more unexpectedly than on the Commodore's eldest born, then enjoying brief leisure in the shadow of the Green Mountain, who rushed back to the city half distraught with anger and fear; for he knew his sister's husband to be deep in these shares, and did *not* know whether the latter had been operating finally for rise or fall.

When the storm was at its wildest, million after million of Central scrip—prepared for this special emergency—was 'floated' into the market; and at each fresh issue, not only the harassed speculators, but the outside public, caught eagerly, as drowning men will clutch at safety-rafts.

Vanderbilt's own profits on this occasion have never been, and probably never will be, accurately known; but, after allowing largely for American grandiloquence, it really seems probable that the like have not been realised at any single stroke recorded in modern commercial history. For, not only was the value of the original shares, of which he was so large a holder, enormously increased, but he had unlimited and almost irresponsible command of the fresh scrip, which instantly was at a high premium. Truly it is no wonder if even in a community accustomed to take such things coolly—

> The boldest held his breath
> For a time.

Perhaps the most remarkable feature in all the strange story, is the fact of this same scrip having paid steady dividends of about six or seven per cent., ever since; and there is talk, I believe—if it be not already accomplished—of converting it into stock. So the Commodore's own coffers were filled to overflowing, without apparently defrauding anyone of his due. A man who could not only achieve, but secure such a victory, must needs leave a deep mark on his time. And this name will long be a household-word; though it may be questioned if in a country lax in its commercial code, and indulgent to success, it will be cherished or honoured.

Temperate and frugal; for tobacco is his sole excess, and a trotting stud his sole extravagance—not a fond husband or father; but never an overt adulterer, and just in his hard way towards his children—scarcely a professing Christian; yet rendering to the Church her dues, and not slow to contribute to public charities—both physically and morally absolutely fearless—prudent, patient, persevering and sagacious—scenting either danger or profit from afar with a keenness allied to instinct. Such civic crowns Vanderbilt may assuredly claim.

Now turn another page.

A despot in council, a bully on the tavern-stoop—everywhere, whether in jest or earnest, a foul-mouthed blasphemous railer—grossly illiterate and boorish, and boastful of both defects—ever morose and saturnine, save when moved to surly laughter by some brutal jest—liberal in bribes, and sometimes ostentatious in benevolence; but the veriest miser of private alms—a man who would liever, any day, hire a sycophant than secure a friend—always utterly remorseless, pitiless, and unrelenting; and, in his arrogant intolerance of rivalry, often wantonly perfidious and cruel.

In the early part of this century flourished, like a mighty bay-tree, a certain Marquis, one of the Regent's chief worthies. He had practised the Seven Sins so sedulously and extensively, that small vices began to pall on his taste; and even in gambling he craved for some adventitious excitement. "It is poor sport playing with rich folks," he was wont to aver; "but I like winning of poor men—*they feel it so.*"

Truly, it would seem as if some of the peculiarities of this amiable noble had been reproduced in the Commodore. That a man of his reticence and reserve should keep his secrets safe locked up, is natural enough; but that he should not seldom mislead his fellows to their hurt, is somewhat unaccountable. He has, ere this given a valuable clue to a bar-keeper, prize-fighter, or trotting-jockey, when his own kin and familiars were groping helplessly in the dark. Indeed, it is credibly affirmed that his son-in-law, after being trapped in divers commercial pit-falls, only escaped ruin, by at last going exactly counter to the Commodore's suggestions; and, ever since, he has stood much higher in the old man's favour, as one who, having paid his 'prentice fees, is entitled to the honour of an independent trader.

Assuredly, there are very many mansions in New York that would still remain closed against this *Roi Carotte*, were his wealth and power trebled. Nevertheless, he is beyond question rather a popular favourite. When, awhile ago, not a month after the death of his first wife, the mother of all his children and his faithful help-meet for forty years, he sold her favourite horse to the highest bidder, people only laughed—saying, "it was the Commodore all over;" and others of his social offences have in like manner been glossed over and condoned.

Well—it little becomes us, who have gathered up reverently the scattered aspirates of railway monarchs, and been edified by fraudulent Gamaliels, to sit in judgment on our neighbours; but, I think, we have never yet bowed down before quite such an idol as this.

We encountered several more celebrities that day, but none of European renown. On the whole, a drive out to Haarlem Lane or the Bloomingdale Road, is about as amusing a way of passing a spring afternoon as can be conceived. Putting horse-flesh entirely aside, the variety of equipages is very wonderful. Some would be quite in place in the Bois or the Row. No American hands taught yonder pair to step and carry themselves so correctly; and even the coachman you might swear was born and bred not a mile from Piccadilly. But this is a recent fashion; and has not prevailed to any extent, even amongst the 'Ten Thousand.' The wagons and buggies, if sometimes unsightly, are invariably well built, and fit for hard, fast work; but some of the heavier vehicles are 'cautions' for clumsiness, and drawn by cattle put together in a manner fearful to behold. Over-tight bearing reins and couplings are quite fatal to fast travelling; but the effect thereof is not so ludicrous as that of two raw-boned garrons, whose top speed is under six miles an hour, struggling along in seeming independence of the pole, whilst this last sways and pitches like the bowsprit of a lively cutter.

Almost all American dragsmen lack 'finish;' but they are safe as a rule, and, at any rate, seldom lack nerve. Amongst the professionals, the coloured persons are decidedly to be preferred: some of these have actually learned to *sit* on their box, and are turned out as correctly as one could desire.

Central Park in itself deserves a visit. When I saw it last, it was the dreariest waste imaginable: now, it might bear comparison with any plaisance abutting on a metropolitan city. For though there can never be any great wealth of foliage, even when the trees lately planted and transplanted come to maturity, the inequalities of the ground have been more happily developed here than even in the Bois de Boulogne. Also there is a sense of air and liberty, very agreeable after the turmoil of the Broadway; whilst to get quite clear of the tramways is a real relief; and there are several points of view worth lingering over, before you come to the quaint wooden hostelry—once a convent, save the mark!—where a halt and 'liquor up' are inevitable.

Altogether, the Empire City improves on acquaintance; albeit there must attach to it one grave disadvantage. Having proved the climate now in winter, spring, and summer, I am unable to conceive it as anything but 'trying;' and this is rather a *leitotes.*

CHAPTER XV.

'HASTE is of the devil'—quoth the Eastern sage; and I think one never realizes more thoroughly the wisdom of the ancient saw, than when travelling in a foreign land wherein one is not quite a stranger. It would have been very pleasant to have gone back at leisure over some old tracks, and mark what changes nine years had wrought. But it was not so to be; and four short days were all that could be spared to Washington and Baltimore.

Much must be allowed for prejudice, no doubt, and I own to having quitted the place in a temper, not improved by four months of solitary durance; nevertheless, I believe many—natives no less than aliens—will back me in affirming that the State Metropolis is about the most comfortless of civilised cities.

No squalor offends you; the other public buildings, without lofty architectural pretensions, are not unworthy of the grand white Colossus throned on the Capitoline hill; many private dwellings, of recent erection, are spacious, solid, and excellently contrived; and, since the introduction of street asphalte, the double nuisance of mud and dust, though not cured, is much abated. In spite of all this, I cannot, even now, fancy the most zealous official feeling himself thoroughly at home here. The normal condition of everything, within doors and without, seems to be one of incessant hurry, confusion, and unrest. Everybody is 'seeking' something; though the objects of pursuit may vary infinitely, from a lucrative appointment down to a meal or a share in a bed-chamber. The Congress-man *per se* is not usually a very pleasant or polite person; indeed, considering how he is harassed, there is much excuse for his shortcomings in courtesy; but he is amiable and attractive compared to the office-hunters and the rest of the camp-following. The carcase must be an atomy indeed that will not, before the breath has fairly left it, draw together a score of strident harpies; and, fighting over the quarry, they spare not, be sure, beak or talon. Within the diplomatic atmosphere you may doubtless breathe more freely; but even here the air is often troubled, and there is seldom perfect peace.

Each hotel is, naturally, the centre of a scramble. When we reached the Arlington House in the early dawn, though we had telegraphed for rooms, Tressilian and myself were fain to be grateful for a small double-bedded garret, whilst a couch was improvised for another of our party in the bath-closet adjoining. However, a bright sky overhead, and a breeze blowing freshly up the Potomac, made amends for much; and our Senator was 'all there' to lionise the strangers. For myself I can aver, that the pleasantest sight Washington showed me that day was a familiar Baltimore face, unaltered from the ancient kindliness.

Early on the following forenoon, under the Senator's auspices, we were 'received' by the President. Albeit prepared for republican simplicity, the informalities of the White House struck us rather forcibly. A sentry strolling to and fro in the outer precincts, expectorating copiously the while, did not interfere with the general *sans-gêne*. Ushers or chamberlains there were none: the Senator merely dropped a word or two in passing to a servant in the outer hall; then, quite unattended, we followed him into a kind of antechamber on the first floor, tenanted by some half-dozen loungers. Hence, for the first time so far as I know, our names were sent in.

After the briefest possible delay, we were inducted into an apartment sufficiently lofty and spacious, but absolutely destitute of pomp or ornaments, most resembling, indeed, an ordinary board-room. At a large oblong table in the centre three or four men were writing busily, of whom one only rose as we entered.

Now a President cannot be hedged with any divinity whatsoever. Indeed, being, as Miss Nipper would say, 'only a temporary,' there is no reason why he should carry more of a presence than a mayor or any other ephemeral dignitary. But I think we strangers were all rather disappointed with the *physique* of the famous Ulysses. We had looked to see features resolute, if somewhat stolid, in expression, and a figure sturdily squared; something, in fine, to remind one of the soldier who 'set his foot down' in such bitter earnest at Richmond leaguer. What we saw was a small, undersized man, with wan face and weary eyes, *pêkin* from head to heel, and palpably not quite at his ease. One would have thought myriads of such inflictions must have case-hardened any diffidence; but he spoke in a shy, subdued voice—rather hesitated over each successive formula of greeting—and then paused, as if waiting for a conversational lead. An awkwardness naturally ensued; for on such occasions ordinary persons, like the courtly huntsmen of the *ancien régime*, feel disinclined to cut out the work, howsoever lamely *Monseigneur* may be mounted. At last the Senator, taking heart of grace, struck in; and the President, once over the first fence, ambled on pretty steadily; expressing his personal regard for the 'old country'—regret at the present complications--confidence in the speedy clearing of the political horizon, and so forth. And he said all this in a solid, placid way, that made you feel as if some substance supported the complimentary froth.

Consideration for the President, no less than for ourselves, made us not seek to prolong the interview; for he looked ill as well as harassed, and we heard afterwards that for some time past he had been rather ailing. The atmosphere of the White House, if it at all resembles that of the audience-chamber, would be very like to promote dyspepsia.* The room, despite its size, was fearfully over-heated, and the air heavy with nicotine; indeed, whilst conversing, the Chief ceased not to twist betwixt his fingers the stump of a big black cigar.

If his outward seeming differed from my ideal, my moral conception of Ulysses Grant, after having seen him face to face, is hardly, if at all, altered. Essentially a substantial man—not easily led, and hardly to be urged, either by persuasion or obloquy, an inch further or faster than it pleases him to advance—upright in his dealings, both public and private, albeit not heedless of the main chance, nor devoid of the spirit of partizanship—in his home policy, careful *quieta non movere*—in his foreign scarcely aggressive, though inclined to take any fair pretext for enlarging American borders. A man whose light is never like to be set on high, like that of some who have preceded him; nevertheless, the longer it burns steadily, the better, I think, it will be for honest folk on either Atlantic shore.

A pleasanter recollection of that forenoon was a visit paid by Tressilian and myself to Charles Sumner. A courteous reception, even if we had

* Vide Appendix E.

not come by invitation, was a matter of course: yet I was agreeably surprised; for, although I have been in his company twice or thrice, long ago, my recollection had not done justice to the great orator's powers of *causerie.* The talk ran chiefly on indifferent topics; but, without constraint or affectation, such could not be invariably adhered to; and it was admirable to mark the tact and delicacy with which our host—never actually evading a difficulty—glided over dangerous ground. Listening to his smooth, facile periods, it was hard to realise that his name could ever have been associated with Indirect Claims. There was nothing strange in this, after all; only the lower order of demagogues are, on and off the platform, pretty nearly the same.

Overwork, rumour affirms, has told heavily on Mr. Sumner. If this be so, the outward and visible signs thereof are faint to discern. Beyond an increase of bulk, and a thorough blanching of the long flowing hair, the past decade seemed to me to have worked few changes. Indeed, the face—perhaps from the filling up of its outlines—appeared to me less worn than when I looked upon it last; but that the labour has been incessant, and the mental strain severe, none would doubt, after glancing at tables literally smothered with *paperasses.* Indeed, our host assured us that the perusal of his correspondence, after it had been carefully sifted, often took him far into the night. The house, though spacious enough for all ordinary requirements, is somewhat strait for the full display of its art treasures. Every available foot of wall, and inch of space, is already occupied; and even the study, specially consecrated to business, reminds you far less of America than of Rome. Minutes, that dragged so heavily at the White House, flitted rapidly here; and I was only just in time to catch the train for Baltimore, whither I went alone; for my comrades, having no old associations to tempt them, elected to spend the residue of their leave in Columbia.

Driving through the streets from the Baltimore depôt, I was struck with the changed aspect of all the surroundings. Even in that feverish war-time trade could not be said to stagnate here; but it was a feeble uncertain flutter, most unlike the business-like bustle which now prevailed. I was not surprised to hear afterwards that the population of the city had increased by nearly a third, and that her commerce was flourishing exceedingly; for direct lines of steamers run hence to the principal European ports, and the port is crowded with general shipping. Generally speaking, the keen mercantile spirit of this people—ever quick at seizing and moulding opportunities—might claim credit for this wondrous progress. But I believe there are cases here, not a few, where men have worked with fiercer earnestness because the whirring of the business-wheels drowned, for a while, bitter voices of the past to which it is wisest not to harken.

My first visit was to the Maryland Club. Here there were few marks of change. Though the society had been somewhat roughly evicted in the last year of the war, things had evidently settled down again; and even the furniture seemed to occupy the old places. In the same sunny corner stood the same vast arm-chair: only the portly form, that used to fill it in nobly, has long since changed substance for shadow. Indeed, though familiar faces were not lacking, I soon learned that there were voids, wide and many, in the goodly company that used to assemble here. On one—perhaps the cheeriest of them all—had lighted the heaviest grief that can befall humanity; and under the roof-tree that sheltered me oftenest in those days there was still more recent mourning.

But not for this, their revel
Those jovial souls forbore.

In truth, it must have been a poor heart that would not have rejoiced over the succulent canvas-backs, the toothsome terrapins, and Sercial, older than the century, yet full of fragrance and flavour, as when it was brought down from the sunniest slope in Madeira.

But a better cordial than even that rare liquor, was the real Maryland welcome awaiting one everywhere. To have kept a place in kindly memories so long, through good and evil report, with a thousand leagues of sea betwixt—we have been thankful, in our time, for lighter mercies than this.

In such a hurried visit it was difficult to form any accurate conclusion. But, though ancient heart-burnings have healed more completely than might have been reckoned on, I fancied that in not a few cases there were traces of vague discontent and political animosity. This set me pondering more gravely than heretofore over a question, concerning which much has been said and written already, but one of such world-wide interest that it can scarcely become trite or wearisome.

How long is the Great Republic like to remain one and undivided?

I am not thinking now of revolt, revolution, or any violent disruption whatsoever; but of natural causes, working evenly towards an inevitable end. I fancy, few foreigners, who trouble themselves to consider the subject, will traverse the States from ocean to ocean, without some such misgivings, inspired—if by naught else—by that very 'vastness' of which our cousins are so prone to boast. Are you aware that more leagues divide New York from San Francisco than lie betwixt Paris and Bagdad? If you realise this, you wonder less at the tone in which a Californian or Missourian is wont to speak of the Down-Easters. In one long day's journey may be compassed the distance between Boston and Baltimore; yet, in many essentials, the proclivities of these two cities differ not less widely than if they were set in diverse hemispheres. To produce disunion it is not necessary that active antipathy should exist. Without thorough sympathy and identity of interests throughout, it is difficult to see how a federation of such proportions can long cohere. Albeit discontent, and even disaffection, may still smoulder in the South, I hold the probabilities of another Southern rising extremely remote. Nevertheless, I believe that many, now past middle age, will live to see several republics established on this continent; not necessarily at enmity with each other, or struggling for pre-eminence except in fair commercial rivalry, and perhaps always ready to make common cause against a foreign foe; but absolutely self-contained, self-governed, and independent.

Surely each large accession of territory must strengthen such probabilities: yet the Northern mind is loth to acknowledge this. With 'annexation' in view, even the wary Ulysses seems sometimes to forget his sober solid self, and is not over-scrupulous concerning his neighbour's landmark. And still the scheme of aggrandisement proceeds. How long Canada is like to hold her own, is entirely matter of opinion; and we will not here pause to inquire. But the fate of Cuba is even now in the balance, and the proximate acquirement of Mexico may be said to have been 'discounted' already; for, in the very heart of that country, a little quiet prospecting has been done; and, when the stars and stripes are once firmly planted there, certain bold speculators will be at no loss where to ply pick and spade. Beyond a doubt, there are many in the States—just and discreet men to boot—who look forward to the day, not far distant, when the entire North American continent will be absorbed in the Great Republic.

I have heard it argued that even then, both in area and in population, for some time to come, the Russian Empire would hold the vantage; and—being exceedingly feeble on figures—I could not wholly controvert this. Nevertheless, I ventured to affirm that the cases are in nowise parallel. Setting aside the Caucasus, ever ruled rather by the sword than the sceptre—within the sweep of the Russian eagle's wing dwell, and for generations to come are like to dwell, great hordes of mere barbarians, bred in habits of blind obedience, and void of real free aspirations, even when, by oppression or their own wild instincts, stirred to revolt. Furthermore, Russia proper, at least, the Czar overawes, not only with hereditary dignity, but with the semi-divine attributes of the Head of a vast hierarchy: if all earthly principalities and powers were swept away, and merged in universal Communism, in certain natures the old *Relligio*, in some shape or another, would still be found throned.

Mark the difference when you have once crossed the Behring Straits. The savage—pure or mixed—may fairly be eliminated from any question of the future; and, whatever may be their other faults, few old-world countries contain a population less 'barbaric' than the United States, as they now stand, or are like to stand. For—except perhaps in the extreme South—absolute ignorance, even among the negroes, has become rather exceptional. But from civilization with all the modern improvements, a certain amount of factiousness unluckily seems inseparable. Education is, doubtless, an excellent thing; but the quick-witted citizen, with the 'Rights of Man' at his finger's end, will be more apt to vex the soul of his ruler than the dullest of boors. I suppose, on a moderate computation, America could furnish forth a well-defined creed for each week in the year; so that the most devoted adherents of any President, present or to come, are scarce likely to regard him with a jot more veneration on the hierarchic score.

On the whole—chimerical as the idea may sound—if that huge fagot of parti-coloured staves is held prominently together, I am inclined to believe it will be in the grasp of an autocracy.

That difficulties, many and great, would hamper any severance, however amicable, is too evident; and, perhaps, not the least of these would be found in the anomalous position of Maryland. Beyond doubt, the current of her sympathies trends in the same direction as heretofore; nor is it ever likely to turn: nevertheless, it is hard to see how the boundary line could touch the Atlantic, otherwise than at the mouth of the Potomac. For, if the territory east of the Missouri were divided under two Republics, it seems as if the District of Columbia must still remain neutral ground, invested with the ancient Elean privileges, and the Capitol the properest meeting-place for federal councils.

I suppose time and patience would solve this puzzle, as they have solved many another; but I would it looked less intricate; for few can have sojourned long in this most genial State without retaining an interest in her future. Though our faces were set fairly homewards now, I felt as if I were leaving much of home-like behind, when, on our way back to New York, we crossed the Susquehanna.

Bright spring weather had come east at last, and we were able, for the first time, to stroll about the Empire City without being forced to wade through snow or mire. That the last few years have much improved and beautified her, it is impossible to deny. The white marble, now profusely employed, produces a wonderfully good effect; especially as, in this climate, its gloss and purity do not soon pass away. Several new stores and hotels are faced with this costly material. In the Roman Catholic cathedral—now about half complete—no meaner stone mingles. If the original plan be carried out, there are few like edifices with which this stately structure will not stand compare. But vast sums have been sunk here already; and, though scarce an Irish labourer grudges a tithe from his daily hire, and wealthy devotees are liberal, the walls mount slowly.

Still—once clear of the Fifth Avenue—wandering about the good town, *Desinit in piscem* will perpetually recur to you. The Broadway remains the same quaint patchwork in brick and mortar; and the contrasts are often more glaring than heretofore. Some recent erections are not only magnificent, but bear evidence of a pure architectural taste; and when, shoulder to shoulder with one of these, you find a hideous *baraque*, plastered over with parti-coloured placards, the effect is simply provoking; albeit a thorough-going Yankee will insist that it is rather picturesque.

Just two short days, into which were pressed the work, and perhaps the wassail, of seven; and we paced the familiar deck of the 'China' once more, with Sandy Hook on our quarter. A perfectly uneventful voyage—yet pleasant as fair weather and fair company could make it—and, on the tenth morning, we heard Birkenhead bells ringing to matin-song.

Now for a brief epilogue, or apology, if you will.

A great traveller remarked a while ago, with equal truth and simplicity, that a "certain amount of egotism was inseparable from personal narrative;" and for this defect I hold it needless to make excuse, inasmuch as the evading it would have entailed much wearisome periphrasis. Furthermore, it may be doubted how far one is justified in putting one's own sentiments into the mouth of others who actually move, live, and have being. I am free to confess that the route we traversed would, under ordinary circumstances, offer no more stirring incidents than might be found betwixt London and the Land's End; and some of our facts are trite as—let us say—the motto on the title-page. Nevertheless, amongst 'things not generally known' are many lying little remote from the world's main highways; and, perhaps, a few matters recorded here would not be found in ordinary guide-books. With no temptation to set down aught in malice, I have striven very earnestly to be swayed neither by friendship nor favour. Any palpably interested statements, unless borne out by strong external evidence, I have put wholly aside, or used them only as counterpoises to others of a like nature; and a glance at the Appendix will show that in figures we have usually undershot the mark.

Ever since Terah and the other patriarchs 'went forth from Ur of the Chaldees to go into the land of Canaan,' a tide of emigration, always swelling in volume, has followed the sun; and—*Kenn'st du das Land?*—is translated into many tongues from the Teuton. Without venturing to answer the query authoritatively, I have tried to suggest where the answer may be found; and if only a few honest yeomen, or stout adventurers, profit by the clue, neither time nor trouble has been wasted.

At the very worst, I shall never regret these latest American wanderings ; for they brought much worth remembering, even if—as just judges should decide—little worth recording.

APPENDIX.

Page 30.—A.

By an odd coincidence, while this sheet was in process of correction, the following appeared in the American column of *The Times* :—

"In the 'Crédit Mobilier' inquiry two former Members of Congress have been found who not only admit having held the stock, but, unlike some of the others who have testified, they resort to no excuses, but boldly say they bought it to make a profit from it, and they deny any man's right to question the propriety of their conduct. These men are James F. Wilson, of Iowa, and Benjamin M. Boyer, of Pennsylvania. Boyer says he only got 100 shares, and regrets that he was not able to get more. The testimony taken shows that the 'Crédit Mobilier' made no less than $30,000,000. This enormous profit was made from the Government bonds and lands, yet it left the Union Pacific Railroad heavily in debt and in arrears to the Government. The Government directors of the line, of whom Brooks is and Wilson was one, ought to have prevented this huge swindle, but the shares they held (although in direct violation of law) sealed their lips. The movement is very strong to have the railroad seized for its debts, and the 'Crédit Mobilier' shareholders sued to get back at least enough of their gains to reimburse the Government its expenditures over and above the actual value of the road."

Page 40.—B.

From the latest report of the Commissioners we gather that the Redskins of all kinds, now existing on American ground, can hardly muster 150,000. The estimate must be partly founded on guess-work; for the numbering of some tribes could hardly be accomplished by any one valuing his scalp. But doubtless it is sufficiently accurate for all practical purposes. Out of these 150,000, more than a third are so far domesticated in their own territory that no more trouble need be looked for here than in any ordinary distant settlement. On the other hand, certain hostile tribes seem, of late, to have plucked up heart and attempted something more than desultory forays. There has been sharp skirmishing down in Arizona; and in Upper California the U.S. troops seem to have been twice decisively worsted. But such reverses are really profitable. Indian fighting would be wonderfully simplified if the savage in any wise be tempted to stand up in fair field. All things considered, the whole question seems to be narrowing itself into a compass strait indeed.

Page 73.—C.

From one cause or another, months have intervened betwixt inditing the first and the last of the preceding pages. It must be confessed that the present prospects of the 'Emma' are hardly so prosperous as when these lines were penned; nevertheless, I am not minded to modify or retract a single letter thereof. The quality of the ore may, of course, vary with each assay; but subsequent reports have only strengthened my conviction that the estimate of quantity, then actually 'exposed,' was in no wise exaggerated. It looks like prophesying after the event, to affirm that the flooding of the mine in this later spring, whilst these vast drifts were melting, suggested itself as a probable danger even to us who scanned things with unprofessional eyes. But, so far as I can learn, the 'cave' which occasioned so much damage and hindrance of work was really attributable rather to surface water, filtering largely through the chinks and pores of the limestone, than to the breaking up of deep hidden springs. This disaster would be included, I suppose, in 'the acts of God,' provided against in bills of lading. But the unlucky 'Emma' fell likewise into the hand of man, in the shape of long litigation; and though she eventually made her case good against the Illinois Company, so far as present cost is concerned it seems to have been rather a Pyrrhic victory. Up to February last every shaft, winze, and driftway had assuredly been driven on the broadest of prospecting principles: hence the exceptional development. How they have been working since, I cannot pretend to say. Eighteen per cent. in monthly dividends on a million sterling, is no light load to carry; and neither mine nor mule can work fairly, if overburdened. Only a constant supply of high-class ore can meet these frequent calls; and the exhaustion of one or two rich veins must interfere with fair exploration. This is what the hill folk mean by 'picking out the eyes of a mine.' I do not affirm that the 'Emma' has been so managed of late; but the temptation—perhaps it would be fairer to say the pressure—is obvious. Probably, ere long, both directors and shareholders may be convinced that these frequent *ad interim* dividends, however attractive in a prospectus, are at variance with sound theories of investment. Furthermore—casting no imputation on our neighbour—it may be questioned whether it is wise to leave the control of American works, supported almost entirely by British capital, exclusively in American hands. An English resident manager might not find it at first an easy post; yet tact and firmness have triumphed over greater obstacles than he would be like to encounter. A superficial knowledge of mineralogy, and the intelligence of an ordinary mining engineer, would not suffice; and he must not alone be bribe-proof, but steeled against fear or favour. You do not light on this sample, perhaps, every day. Nevertheless, not a few such are to the fore in flesh and blood; and, with millions at stake, they are surely worth the seeking.

D.

Within the last fortnight I have read—not yet thoroughly enough, I must own—"California, a Book for Travellers and Settlers," by Charles Nordhoff. It is carefully and exhaustively written; though the chapters on colonization appear rather addressed to native than foreign emigrants. But it is a rather costly work; and, like many others published beyond the Atlantic, will probably not obtain here circulation wide as it deserves. Therefore, I am glad to supplement my scanty knowledge by infinitely larger experience, especially as it more than confirms all the facts stated above. To practical farmers the concluding extract may seem worth attentive perusal; for it gives, in a small space a very comprehensive notion of husbandry in Middle California.

ı. (1), page 191.

"It is a singular piece of good fortune to the farmers and land-owners, that they got a remarkably fine season and the railroad in the same year. They have known how to avail themselves of their good luck, for they have put in enormous crops. One of the best informed men in Stockton assured me that the San Joaquin Valley will send to tide-water, in the year 1872, 180,000 tons of wheat. Mr. Friedlander, the great grain buyer of this State, is reported to me to have estimated the probable export of the whole State this year at 700,000 tons.

D. (2), page 192.

"One irrigation company is already at work in the San Joaquin country upon a large scale; it has forty miles of canal dug, and a large force of men is now at work extending this canal. The plan of this company contemplates not only irrigation, but incidentally the reclamation of a million of acres of swamp and overflowed lands.

D. (3), page 193.

"Between Stockton and Merced lie about six hundred square miles of wheat. The railroad train runs through what appears to be an interminable wheat-field, with small houses and barns at great distances apart, and no fences, except those by which the company has guarded its trains against the cattle, which are turned into the fields after harvest to glean the grain and consume the stubble.

"Wheat, wheat, wheat, and nothing but wheat, is what you see on your journey, as far as the eye can reach over the plain in every direction. Fields of two, three, and four thousand acres make but small farms; here is a man who 'has in' 20,000 acres; here one with 40,000 acres, and another with some still more preposterous amount—all in wheat.

D. (4), page 195.

"Miller and Lux own forty miles of land on the western side of the San Joaquin, and other persons own almost equally great tracts. Mr. Miller is the possessor of half a million of acres in this State; he has nearly 100,000 cattle; and, being a shrewd business man, he is fencing in his great estate, to reserve it for his own cattle. He is eager for more land; and is said to have determined that he will not rest until he can drive his cattle over his own land from Los Angeles to the Sacramento.

D. (5), page 199.

"Los Angeles is, at present, the centre of the orange culture in this State. The tree grows well in all Southern California, wherever water can be had for irrigation.

"Sixty orange trees are commonly planted to the acre. They may be safely transplanted at three or even four years, if care is used to keep the air from the roots. They grow from seed; and it is believed in California that grafting does not change or improve the fruit. It begins to bear in from six to eight years from the seed, and yields a crop for market at ten years. With good thorough culture and irrigation, it is a healthy tree; if it is neglected, or if the gopher has gnawed its roots, the scale insect appears; but a diseased tree is very rarely seen in the orchards.

"At from ten to twelve years from the seed the tree usually bears 1000 oranges, and they are selling now in San Francisco for from fifteen to thirty-five thousand dollars per 1000.

"I have satisfied myself, by examination of nearly all the bearing orchards in the southern counties, and by comparing the evidence of their owners, that at fifteen years from the seed, or twelve years from the planting of three-year old trees, an orange orchard which has been faithfully cared for, and is favourably situated, will bear an average of 1000 oranges to the tree. This would give, at twenty dollars per 1000—a low average—a product of 1200 dollars per acre.

"One man can care for twenty acres of such an orchard; and every other expense, including picking, boxes, shipping, and commissions in San Francisco, is covered by five dollars per 1000. The net profit per acre would, therefore, be a trifle less than 900 dollars.

D. (6), page 205.

"The price of land at first strikes the stranger as high. Near Los Angeles they ask from thirty to a hundred dollars per acre for unimproved farming land. I thought they were already discounting the railroad which is coming to them, and which will no doubt cause this part of the country to increase rapidly in population and wealth. Everybody was 'talking railroad.' A corps of engineers of the Southern Pacific Company was near the town completing surveys for the road; and as I had seen in the East the rise in prices following the mere announcement of a new railroad, it was natural for me to think that prices here had been affected by the same cause. But I am satisfied that they are, on the whole, not too high.

"The Congress land which remains unoccupied in this and the adjoining counties has been reserved from sale until the Southern Pacific Railroad line is determined, and that company, which works, I believe, with the help of a land grant, shall have located its alternate sections. There is, I am told, a great deal of good land in this part of the public domain—how much I am unable to tell. The soil in this country is mostly a rich, loose, sandy loam, with patches of *adobe*, which is a stiff black clay, and forms, with proper cultivation, the very richest grain land of California. It is on the *adobe* soil about Watsonville and Santa Cruz that the enormous crops of wheat have grown; some farms averaging, for several years in succession, from seventy to eighty bushels of wheat per acre.

D. (7), page 207.

"They sow the wheat here from the 1st of December to the 1st of March, and they have another three months to harvest it in, with a certainty that no rain will disturb them during their long harvest.

"The fields are ploughed with what are called gang-ploughs, which are simply four, six, or eight ploughshares fastened to a stout frame of wood. On the lighter soil eight horses draw a seven-gang plough, and one such team is counted on to put in 640 acres of wheat in the sowing season, or from eight to ten acres per day. Captain Gray, near Merced, has put in this season 4000 acres with five such teams—his own land and his own teams.

"A seed-sower is fastened in front of the plough. It scatters the seed, the ploughs cover it, and the work is done. The plough has no handles, and the ploughman is, in fact, only a driver; he guides the team; the ploughs do their own work. It is easy work, and a smart boy, if his legs are equal to the walk, is as good a ploughman as anybody; for the team is trained to turn the corners at the driver's word, and the plough is not handled at all.

"It is a striking sight to see, as I saw, ten eight-horse teams following each other in over a vast plain cutting 'lands' a mile long, and, when all had passed me, leaving a track forty feet wide of ploughed ground.

"On the heavier soil the process is somewhat different. An eight-horse team moves a four-gang plough, and gets over about six acres per day. The seed is then sown by a machine which scatters it forty feet, and sows from seventy-five to one hundred acres in a day, and the ground is then harrowed and cross-harrowed.

"When the farmer, in this valley, has done his winter sowing, he turns his teams and men into other ground, which he is to summer fallow. This he can do from the 1st of March to the middle of May; and by it he secures a remunerative crop for the following year, even if the season is dry. This discovery is of inestimable importance to the farmers on the drier part of these great plains. Experience has now demonstrated conclusively, that if they plough their land in the spring, let it lie until the winter rains come on, then sow their wheat promptly and harrow it in, they are sure of a crop; and the summer will have killed every weed besides.

"After the summer fallowing is done, the teams have a rest. The horses and mules are turned out to grass until the 4th of July, when the harvest begins.

"It is then the rainless season, and the farmer gets his teams, his headers, his grain waggons, his thresher, and his sacks and men into the field, and on the light soil cuts, threshes, and puts into sacks the grain at the rate often of one hundred and fifty acres per day.

"Three 'headers,' which cut off only the heads of the wheat stalks, leaving the straw standing, and nine wagons to take the heads from the headers to the thresher, require to work them twenty-three men and eighty-three horses. With this force they got in one hundred and fifty acres per day. The grain, put into sacks, is left on the fields until time and teams can be got to haul it to the railroad, or often until it is sold. It does not sweat nor mould, and there is no fear of rain.

"As soon as the crop is harvested, the teams are hitched to a brush—six horses to a twenty-foot brush, which goes over the field at the rate of forty acres per day. This brush scatters the grain which has been dropped in the fields; and sometimes a little more seed is added. When it has been brushed in, it is ploughed—two or three inches deep—to cover the seed; and from this comes, without further care, what is called a 'volunteer' crop, which is often better than the first, and is certainly counted on.

"Now the horses and men have another interval of rest until the rains begin and ploughing recommences.

"Thus, as one farmer pointed out to me, they have work for their teams almost the whole year, and have no horses eating their heads off in idleness.

"In the heavier soils, the 'volunteer' crop is put in with the harrow instead of the brush; and this is followed by a 'chisel cultivator,' having from seven to thirteen teeth, four inches deep. If these leave the ground rough, it is again harrowed.

"At five bushels per acre, if wheat brought two dollars and a half a hundred pounds, the farmer on these sandy plains makes three dollars and a half per acre, clear of every expense. This result, which seemed to me incredible, I saw demonstrated by figures of the cost of the crop which were satisfactory to a whole roomful of farmers.

"But if you will remember that it is no uncommon thing for a farmer to put in three or four thousand acres, you will see what money they make, even with a small crop, if the price happens to be good, as it often is in a bad year. Two and a half cents is, of course, a high price, and a cent and a quarter is a more usual price in good years. But at that rate a crop of ten bushels per acre pays so well on the sandy plains that farmers down here count confidently on making large fortunes this year.

"I was fortunate enough to find myself one afternoon among a dozen farmers, some having sandy soil, and some the heavier loam; and, after discussing the comparative cost of cultivation, which is nearly double on the heavy land, and the product, which is as ten bushels to from twenty to twenty-five, I listened to an earnest argument concerning the relative merits of sand and clay.

"A very intelligent man, who owned and worked 2000 acres of clay and loam, said, at the close of the discussion, 'The sand has many merits; it can be worked very cheaply, and it bears drought surprisingly well; but after all it is only good for wheat; it must always be farmed on a large scale, and circumstances may make it unprofitable some day; whereas on the clay we can raise anything we like, and are not dependent on wheat alone.' He added, 'The clay and loam farms will have to be cut up, and will be before many years. It will pay better on that land to take one hundred and sixty acres and work it in various crops thoroughly, than to exhaust 2000 or 3000 acres by skimming over the surface.'

"I told you much of the land is rented. It is customary in such cases for the land-owner to furnish seed, feed for the teams, all the tools and machinery needed for putting in and harvesting the crops, and the land and necessary buildings, and he gets half the crop put in bags on the field, and furnishes the bags for his share. The renter, as the tenant is called, furnishes only the teams and men, the supplies for the men, and his own grain-bags.

"This arrangement is not inequitable; and it gives, as you will see, an important advantage to a man without capital. An eight-horse team is worth about six hundred dollars; with five such teams, and five men—who receive in the winter thirty dollars per month and rations—4000 acres can be put into wheat.

"When the work is done, the teams can be hired out, or they can be turned into pastures without cost. I was not surprised to hear that many men have become rich as renters. Two or three good crops enable a renter to buy a large tract of his own."

Page 234.—E.

"A PRESIDENTIAL MANSION.—Major Badcock, in charge of the public grounds in Washington, has made a report on the 'White House,' and states that the President's family are confined to a small number of badly-arranged rooms on the second floor, without closets or clothes-presses, with one inconvenient bath-room, without the possibility of running water in the dressing-rooms, with no private entrance, and, when the family are all at home, without even one guest-chamber. The ceilings of the rooms are dangerously cracked, the floor timbers are rotted and rotting, and the floors are settled several inches. The basement and servants' rooms are below the level of the ground and excessively damp and unhealthy, so that since the spring of 1869 three persons employed in the executive mansion have died of pneumonia, while the whole house is peculiarly exposed to malaria."—*Morning Post, Feb. 21st.*

THE END.

BRADBURY, AGNEW, & CO., PRINTERS, WHITEFRIARS.

Chapman and Hall's

CATALOGUE OF BOOKS;

INCLUDING

BOOKS FOR THE USE OF SCHOOLS,

ISSUED UNDER THE AUTHORITY OF

The Science and Art Department, South Kensington.

193, Piccadilly, London,
January, 1873.

NEW NOVELS.

EUSTACE DIAMONDS. By ANTHONY TROLLOPE.
Three Vols.

TEN YEARS. By GERTRUDE YOUNG. Two Vols.
[*In January.*

WILD WEATHER. By LADY WOOD. Two Vols.
[*In the Press.*

CAPTAIN O'SHAUGHNESSY'S SPORTING CAREER. **An Autobiography. Two Vols.** [*In January.*

BRIGHT MORNING. By M. GRANT. Two Vols.
[*In the Press.*

THOMAS CARLYLE'S WORKS.

PEOPLE'S EDITION.

The Publishers of Mr. CARLYLE'S Works, in deference to the strong desire generally expressed by great numbers of the purchasers of the PEOPLE'S EDITION that it should include the whole of the Writings of Mr. CARLYLE, have much pleasure in announcing that arrangements have been made for continuous issue, in Two-Shilling Volumes.

Already Published.

SARTOR RESARTUS. 1 vol., with Portrait of Mr. Carlyle. Thirty-five Thousand *of this Edition have been issued.*

THE FRENCH REVOLUTION. 3 vols.

LIFE OF JOHN STERLING. 1 vol.

OLIVER CROMWELL'S LETTERS AND SPEECHES. 5 vols.

HERO-WORSHIP. 1 vol.

PAST AND PRESENT. 1 vol.

CRITICAL AND MISCELLANEOUS ESSAYS. 7 vols.

THE LATTER-DAY PAMPHLETS.

To be followed by

THE LIFE OF SCHILLER, and
THE LIFE OF FREDERICK THE GREAT.

CHARLES DICKENS'S WORKS.

HOUSEHOLD EDITION.

Now Publishing,

IN WEEKLY PENNY NUMBERS AND SIXPENNY MONTHLY PARTS.

Each Penny Number will contain Two Illustrations.

OLIVER TWIST. With 28 Illustrations, cloth gilt, 2*s.* 6*d.*; in paper covers, 1*s.* 6*d.*

MARTIN CHUZZLEWIT. With 59 Illustrations, cloth gilt, 4*s.*; in paper covers, 3*s.*

DAVID COPPERFIELD. With 60 Illustrations and a Portrait, cloth gilt, 4*s.* paper covers, 3*s.*

BLEAK HOUSE is now being issued.

Messrs. CHAPMAN & HALL trust that by this Edition they will be enabled to place the Works of the most popular British Author of the present day in the hands of all English readers.

New Publications.

AUSTRALIA, AND NEW ZEALAND.

By ANTHONY TROLLOPE.

2 vols., demy 8vo.

[In January.

THE SECOND VOLUME OF

THE LIFE OF CHARLES DICKENS.

1842—1852.

By JOHN FORSTER.

With Portraits and Illustrations. Price 14s.

THE LIFE OF ROUSSEAU.

By JOHN MORLEY.

[In the press.

THE TRUE CROSS. A Poem.

By G. J. WHYTE-MELVILLE.

[In January.

JEST AND EARNEST:

A Collection of Reviews and Essays.

By G. WEBBE DASENT, D.C.L.

2 vols., post 8vo.

[In January.

SIX YEARS IN EUROPE.

By MADAME KIBRIZLI-MEHEMET-PASHA,

Author of "Thirty Years in the Harem."

[In January.

THE MANNERS, CUSTOMS, AND COSTUMES OF THE MIDDLE AGES.

By PAUL LACROIX.

Illustrated with Fifteen Chromo-lithographs, and 440 Wood Engravings.

1 vol., royal 8vo. [*In the press.*

OLD COURT LIFE OF FRANCE.

By MRS. ELLIOT,

Author of "The Diary of an Idle Woman in Italy," &c.

In 2 vols., demy 8vo. [*In January.*

THE CAUSE, DATE, AND DURATION OF THE LAST GLACIAL EPOCH OF GEOLOGY.

With an Investigation of a New Movement of the Earth.

By LIEUT.-COL. DRAYSON, R.A., F.R.A.S.

Demy 8vo. [*In January.*

RECOLLECTIONS OF CANADA.

By LIEUT.-COL. MARTINDALE, C.B. With numerous Illustrations by LIEUT. CARLISLE, R.A.

ROME.

By FRANCIS WEY. W th an Introduction by W. W. STORY.

Containing 345 beautiful Illustrations. Forming a magnificent Volume in sup. royal 4to. Price £3, in cloth.

THE OCEAN, THE ATMOSPHERE, AND LIFE.

By ÉLISÉE RECLUS.

With 207 Illustrations and 27 Coloured Maps. 2 vols., demy 8vo. Price 26*s.*

Forming the Second Series of "THE EARTH." A Descriptive History of the Phenomena and Life of the Globe.

OTHER COUNTRIES.

By MAJOR WILLIAM MORRISON BELL.

2 Vols., demy, with Illustrations and Maps. 30*s.*

TO THE CAPE FOR DIAMONDS.

By FREDERICK BOYLE.

Post 8vo. 14*s.*

A PRACTICAL MANUAL OF CHEMICAL ANALYSIS AND ASSAYING.

As applied to the Manufacture of Iron from its Ores, and to Cast Iron, Wrought Iron, and Steel, as found in Commerce.

By L. L. DE KONINCK, Dr. Sc., and E. DIETZ. Edited with Notes by ROBERT MALLET, F.R.S., F.G.S., &c.

Crown 8vo. 6*s.*

PARABLES AND TALES.

By THOMAS GORDON HAKE. With Illustrations by ARTHUR HUGHES.

Crown 8vo.

VOLTAIRE.

By JOHN MORLEY.

New Edition. Crown 8vo. Price 6*s.*

THE HUMAN RACE.

By LOUIS FIGUIER.

With 243 Engravings on Wood, and Eight Chromo-lithographs. Demy 8vo. Price 18*s.*

RABIES AND HYDROPHOBIA.

By GEORGE FLEMING, F.R.G.S.

With Illustrations. Demy 8vo. Price 15*s.*

THE HISTORY OF ENGLAND FROM 1830.

By WILLIAM NASSAU MOLESWORTH.

Vols. I. and II. Demy 8vo. Price 15s. each. Vol. III.—completing the Work—*in January.*

TRAVELS IN INDO-CHINA AND IN CHINA.

By LOUIS DE CARNÉ,

Member of the Commission of Exploration of the Mekong. Demy 8vo, with Map and Illustrations. Price 16s.

In Two Handsome Volumes. Price £4 4s.

THE KERAMIC GALLERY,

Comprising about Six Hundred Illustrations of rare, curious, and choice examples of Pottery and Porcelain, from the Earliest Times to the Present, selected by the Author from the British Museum, the South Kensington Museum, the Geological Museum, and various Private Collections. With Historical Notices and Descriptions.

By WILLIAM CHAFFERS,

Author of "Marks and Monograms on Pottery and Porcelain," "Hall Marks on Plate." &c.

THE LIFE OF OLIVER GOLDSMITH.

By JOHN FORSTER.

Fifth Edition. With additional Notes, original Illustrations by MACLISE, STANFIELD, LEECH, DOYLE, several additional designs, and two beautifully engraved Portraits from the Original Painting by REYNOLDS and from the Statue by FOLEY. In 2 vols. Price 21s.

SIR JOHN ELIOT:

A BIOGRAPHY.

By JOHN FORSTER.

A New and Popular Edition, with Portraits. In 2 Vols. Price 14s.

WALTER SAVAGE LANDOR:

A BIOGRAPHY.

By JOHN FORSTER.

New and Cheaper Edition, with Portraits. In 1 Vol. [*In the press.*

PRACTICAL HORSE-SHOEING.

By G. FLEMING, F.R.G.S., &c.

8vo. Sewed. With Illustrations. Price 2s.

[*New Edition in the press.*

MR. THOMAS CARLYLE'S WORKS.

THE LIBRARY EDITION COMPLETE IN THIRTY-THREE VOLUMES.

Demy 8vo, with Portraits and Maps.

A GENERAL INDEX TO THE ABOVE. In One Vol., demy 8vo. Price 6s.

THE EARTH.

A DESCRIPTIVE HISTORY OF THE PHENOMENA AND LIFE OF THE GLOBE.

By ÉLISEE RECLUS.

Translated by the late B. B. WOODWARD, and Edited by HENRY WOODWARD.

With 234 Maps and Illustrations, and 24 page Maps printed in colours.

2 vols. large demy 8vo. 26s.

RECORDS OF THE KING'S OWN BORDERERS

OR OLD EDINBURGH REGIMENT.

EDITED BY CAPTAIN R. T. HIGGINS.

Demy 8vo. 16s.

WHYTE-MELVILLE'S WORKS.

Cheap Edition in Two-Shilling Vols., fancy boards, or 2s. 6d. in cloth.

THE WHITE ROSE.

CERISE. A Tale of the Last Century.

THE BROOKES OF BRIDLEMERE.

"BONES AND I;" or, The Skeleton at Home.

SONGS AND VERSES.

MARKET HARBOROUGH; or, How Mr. Sawyer went to the Shires.

CONTRABAND; or, a Losing Hazard.

M. OR N.—Similia Similibus Curantur.

SARCHEDON. A Legend of the Great Queen.

BOOKS

PUBLISHED BY

CHAPMAN AND HALL.

ABD-EL-KADER. A Biography. Written from dictation by COLONEL CHURCHILL. With fac-simile letter. Post 8vo, 9*s.*

ALL THE YEAR ROUND. Conducted by CHARLES DICKENS. First Series. 20 vols., royal 8vo, cloth, 5*s.* 6*d.* each.

——— New Series. Vols. 1 to 8, royal 8vo, cloth, 5*s.* 6*d.* each.

——— The Christmas Numbers, in 1 vol. royal 8vo. Boards, 2*s.* 6*d.*; cloth, 3*s.* 6*d.*

AUSTIN (ALFRED)—THE GOLDEN AGE. A Satire. Plain, 8vo, cloth, 7*s.*

AUSTRALIAN MEAT—RECEIPTS FOR COOKING. Plain, 8vo, sewed, 6*d.*

AUSTRO-HUNGARIAN EMPIRE AND THE POLICY OF COUNT BEUST. A Political Sketch of Men and Events from 1866 to 1870. By an ENGLISHMAN. Second Edition. Demy 8vo, with Maps. 9*s.*

BELL (DR. W. A.)—NEW TRACKS IN NORTH AMERICA. A Journal of Travel and Adventure, whilst engaged in the Survey of a Southern Railroad to the Pacific Ocean, during 1867—8. With twenty Chromos and numerous Woodcuts. Second edition, demy 8vo, 18*s.*

BELL (MAJOR W. MORRISON)—OTHER COUNTRIES. *With Illustrations and Maps.* 2 vols., 8vo, cloth, 30*s.*

BENSON'S (W.) PRINCIPLES OF THE SCIENCE OF COLOUR. Small 4to, cloth, 15*s.*

BENSON'S (W.) MANUAL OF THE SCIENCE OF COLOUR. *Coloured Frontispiece and Illustrations.* 12mo, cloth, 2*s.* 6*d.*

BLYTH (COLONEL)—THE WHIST-PLAYER. With Coloured Plates of "Hands." Third edition, imp. 16mo, cloth, 5*s.*

BOLTON (M. P. W.)—INQUISITIO PHILOSOPHICA; an Examination of the Principles of Kant and Hamilton. New Edition. Demy 8vo, cloth, 8*s.* 6*d.*

—— EXAMINATION OF THE PRINCIPLES OF THE SCOTO-OXONIAN PHILOSOPHY. New Edition. Demy 8vo, cloth, 5*s.*

BOWDEN (REV. J.)—NORWAY, ITS PEOPLE, PRODUCTS, AND INSTITUTIONS. Crown 8vo, 7*s.* 6*d.*

BOYLE (FREDERICK)—TO THE CAPE FOR DIAMONDS. Post 8vo, cloth.

BRACKENBURY (CAPTAIN, C.B.)—FOREIGN ARMIES AND HOME RESERVES. Republished by special permission from the *Times.* Crown 8vo, cloth, 5*s.*

BRADLEY (THOMAS), of the Royal Military Academy, Woolwich—ELEMENTS OF GEOMETRICAL DRAWING. In two Parts, with Sixty Plates, oblong folio, half bound, each part, 16*s.*

—— Selection (from the above) of Twenty Plates, for the use of the Royal Military Academy, Woolwich. Oblong folio, half bound, 16*s.*

BUCHANAN (ROBERT)—THE LAND OF LORNE; including the Cruise of "The Tern" to the Outer Hebrides. 2 vols., post 8vo, cloth, 21*s.*

BUCKMASTER (J. C.)—THE ELEMENTS OF MECHANICAL PHYSICS. With numerous Illustrations, fcap. 8vo, cloth.

BURCHETT (R.)—LINEAR PERSPECTIVE, for the Use of Schools of Art. 16th Thousand, with Illustrations, post 8vo, cloth, 7*s.*

—— PRACTICAL GEOMETRY, the Course of Construction of Plane Geometrical Figures, with 137 Diagrams. Fourteenth edition, post 8vo, cloth, 5*s.*

—— DEFINITIONS OF GEOMETRY. New edition, 24mo, cloth, 5*d.*

CALDER (ALEXANDER)—THE MAN OF THE FUTURE. Demy, 8vo, cloth, 9*s.*

CARLYLE (DR.)—DANTE'S DIVINE COMEDY.—Literal Prose Translation of THE INFERNO, with Text and Notes. Post 8vo. Second Edition. 14*s.*

THOMAS CARLYLE'S WORKS.

LIBRARY EDITION COMPLETE.

Handsomely printed in 34 vols., demy 8vo, cloth.

SARTOR RESARTUS. The Life and Opinions of Herr Teufelsdrockh. With a Portrait, 7*s.* 6*d.*

THE FRENCH REVOLUTION: A History. 3 vols., each 9*s.*

LIFE OF FREDERICK SCHILLER AND EXAMINATION OF HIS WRITINGS. With Portrait and Plates, 7*s.* 6*d.*

CRITICAL AND MISCELLANEOUS ESSAYS. 6 vols., each 9*s.*

ON HEROES, HERO WORSHIP, AND THE HEROIC IN HISTORY. With a Portrait, 7*s.* 6*d.*

PAST AND PRESENT. With a Portrait, 9*s.*

OLIVER CROMWELL'S LETTERS AND SPEECHES. With Portraits, 5 vols., each 9*s.*

LATTER-DAY PAMPHLETS. 9*s.*

LIFE OF JOHN STERLING. With Portrait, 9*s.*

HISTORY OF FREDERICK THE SECOND. 10 vols., each 9*s.*

TRANSLATIONS FROM THE GERMAN. 3 vols., each 9*s.*

GENERAL INDEX TO THE LIBRARY EDITION. 8vo, cloth, 6*s.*

CHEAP AND UNIFORM EDITION.

In 23 Vols., crown 8vo, cloth.

THE FRENCH REVOLUTION: A History. In 2 vols., 12*s.*

OLIVER CROMWELL'S LETTERS AND SPEECHES, with Elucidations, &c. 3 vols., 18*s.*

LIVES OF SCHILLER AND JOHN STERLING. 1 vol., 6*s.*

CRITICAL AND MISCELLANEOUS ESSAYS. 4 vols., 1*l.* 4*s.*

SARTOR RESARTUS AND LECTURES ON HEROES. 1 vol., 6*s.*

LATTER-DAY PAMPHLETS, 1 vol., 6*s.*

CHARTISM AND PAST AND PRESENT. 1 vol., 6*s.*

TRANSLATIONS FROM THE GERMAN OF MUSÆUS, TIECK, & RICHTER. 1 vol., 6*s.*

WILHELM MEISTER, by Göthe, a Translation, 2 vols., 12*s.*

HISTORY OF FRIEDRICH THE SECOND, called Frederick the Great. Vols. I. & II., containing Part I.—"Friedrich till his Accession." 14*s.*—Vols. III. & IV., containing Part II.—"The First Two Silesian Wars." 14*s.*—Vols. V., VI., VII., completing the Work, 1*l.* 1*s.*

PEOPLE'S EDITION.

CONSISTS OF THE FOLLOWING VOLUMES.

In small crown 8vo. Price 2s. each Vol. bound in cloth.

SARTOR RESARTUS. 2*s.*

FRENCH REVOLUTION. 3 Vols. 6*s.*

LIFE OF JOHN STERLING. 2*s.*

OLIVER CROMWELL'S LETTERS AND SPEECHES. 5 Vols. 10*s.*

ON HEROES AND HERO WORSHIP. 2*s.*

PAST AND PRESENT. 2*s.*

CRITICAL AND MISCELLANEOUS ESSAYS. 7 Vols. 14*s.*

LATTER-DAY PAMPHLETS.

FREDERICK THE GREAT. [*In the press.*

LIFE OF SCHILLER. [*In the press.*

CARLYLE (THOMAS), PASSAGES SELECTED FROM HIS WRITINGS. With Memoir. By THOMAS BALLANTYNE. Second Edition. Crown 8vo, 6s.

—— SHOOTING NIAGARA: AND AFTER? Crown 8vo, sewed, 6*d.*

CRAIK (GEORGE LILLIE)—ENGLISH OF SHAKESPEARE. Illustrated in a Philological Commentary on his Julius Cæsar. Fourth Edition. Post 8vo, cloth, 5s.

—— OUTLINES OF THE HISTORY OF THE ENGLISH LANGUAGE. Eighth Edition. Post 8vo, cloth, 2s. 6d.

DANTE.—DR. J. A. CARLYLE'S LITERAL PROSE TRANSLATION OF THE INFERNO, with the Text and Notes. Second Edition. Post 8vo, 14s.

DASENT (G. WEBBE)—JEST AND EARNEST. A Collection of Reviews and Essays. 2 Vols., post 8vo, cloth.

D'AUMALE (LE DUC)—THE MILITARY INSTITUTIONS OF FRANCE. By H.R.H. The DUC D'AUMALE. Translated with the Author's consent by Captain Ashe, King's Dragoon Guards. Post 8vo, 6s.

D'AZEGLIO—RECOLLECTIONS OF THE LIFE OF MASSINO D'AZEGLIO. Translated, with an Introduction and Notes, by COUNT MAFFEI. 2 vols., post 8vo, 1*l.* 4s.

DE CARNÉ (LOUIS, Member of the Commission of Exploration of the Mekong)—TRAVELS IN INDO-CHINA AND THE CHINESE EMPIRE. 8vo, cloth, 16s.

DE COIN (COLONEL ROBERT L.)—HISTORY AND CULTIVATION OF COTTON AND TOBACCO. Post 8vo, cloth, 9s.

DE LA CHAPELLE (COUNT)—THE WAR OF 1870. Events and Incidents of the Battle Field. Post 8vo, cloth, 4s. 6*d.*

DE GUÉRIN (MAURICE AND EUGÉNIE). A Monograph. By HARRIET PARR, Author of "Essays in the Silver Age," &c., crown 8vo, cloth, 6s.

DIXON (W. HEPWORTH)—THE HOLY LAND. Fourth Edition, with 2 Steel and 12 Wood Engravings, post 8vo, 10s. 6d.

DRAMATISTS OF THE PRESENT DAY. By Q. *Reprinted from the* "Athenæum." Post 8vo, cloth, 4s.

DRAYSON (LIEUT.-COL. A. W.)—THE CAUSE, DATE, AND DURATION OF THE LAST GLACIAL EPOCH OF GEOLOGY, with an investigation of a new movement of the Earth. Demy 8vo, cloth. [*In the press.*

—— PRACTICAL MILITARY SURVEYING AND SKETCHING. Third edition. Post 8vo, cloth, 4s. 6*d.*

CHARLES DICKENS'S WORKS.

ORIGINAL EDITIONS.

THE MYSTERY OF EDWIN DROOD. With Illustrations by S. L. Fildes, and a Portrait engraved by Baker. 8vo, 7*s*. 6*d*. cloth.

OUR MUTUAL FRIEND. With Forty Illustrations by Marcus Stone. Demy 8vo, cloth, 1*l*. 1*s*.

THE PICKWICK PAPERS. With Forty-three Illustrations by Seymour and 'Phiz.' Demy 8vo, cloth, 1*l*. 1*s*.

NICHOLAS NICKLEBY. With Forty Illustrations by 'Phiz.' Demy 8vo, cloth, 1*l*. 1*s*.

SKETCHES BY 'BOZ.' With Forty Illustrations by George Cruikshank. Demy 8vo, cloth, 1*l*. 1*s*.

MARTIN CHUZZLEWIT. With Forty Illustrations by 'Phiz.' Demy 8vo, cloth, 1*l*. 1*s*.

DOMBEY AND SON. With Forty Illustrations by 'Phiz.' Demy 8vo, cloth, 1*l*. 1*s*.

DAVID COPPERFIELD. With Forty Illustrations by 'Phiz.' Demy 8vo, cloth, 1*l*. 1*s*.

BLEAK HOUSE. With Forty Illustrations by 'Phiz.' Demy 8vo, cl., 1*l*. 1*s*.

LITTLE DORRIT. With Forty Illustrations by 'Phiz.' Demy 8vo, cl., 1*l*. 1*s*.

OLIVER TWIST AND TALE OF TWO CITIES. In One Volume. Demy 8vo, cloth, 21*s*.

OLIVER TWIST. With Twenty-four Illustrations. Demy 8vo, cloth, 11*s*.

A TALE OF TWO CITIES. With Sixteen Illustrations by 'Phiz.' Demy 8vo, cloth, 9*s*.

HARD TIMES. Small 8vo, cloth, 5*s*.

THE UNCOMMERCIAL TRAVELLER. Crown 8vo, cloth, 6*s*.

THE OLD CURIOSITY SHOP. With Seventy-five Illustrations by George Cattermole and H. K. Browne. A New Edition. Demy 8vo, uniform with the other Volumes, 21*s*.

BARNABY RUDGE: a Tale of the Riots of 'Eighty. With Seventy-eight Illustrations by G. Cattermole and H. K. Browne. Demy 8vo, uniform with the other Volumes, 21*s*.

CHRISTMAS BOOKS: containing—The Christmas Carol; The Cricket on the Hearth: The Chimes; The Battle of Life; The Haunted House. With all the original Illustrations. Demy 8vo, cloth, 12*s*.

CHARLES DICKENS'S WORKS—*continued.*

ILLUSTRATED LIBRARY EDITION.

With the Original Illustrations, 26 vols., post 8vo, cloth, £10 8s.

				£	s.	d.
Pickwick Papers	With 43	Illustrns.,	2 vols.	0	16	0
Nicholas Nickleby	With 39	„	2 vols.	0	16	0
Martin Chuzzlewit	With 40	„	2 vols.	0	16	0
Old Curiosity Shop *and* Reprinted Pieces	With 36	„	2 vols.	0	16	0
Barnaby Rudge *and* Hard Times	With 36	„	2 vols.	0	16	0
Bleak House	With 40	„	2 vols.	0	16	0
Little Dorrit	With 40	„	2 vols.	0	16	0
Dombey and Son	With 38	„	2 vols.	0	16	0
David Copperfield	With 38	„	2 vols.	0	16	0
Our Mutual Friend	With 40	„	2 vols.	0	16	0
Sketches by Boz	With 39	„	1 vol.	0	8	0
Oliver Twist	With 24	„	1 vol.	0	8	0
Christmas Books	With 17	„	1 vol.	0	8	0
A Tale of Two Cities	With 16	„	1 vol.	0	8	0
Great Expectations	With 8	„	1 vol.	0	8	0
Pictures from Italy *and* American Notes	With 8	„	1 vol.	0	8	0

THE "CHARLES DICKENS" EDITION.

In 19 vols. Crown 8vo, cloth, with Illustrations, £3 2s. 6d.

Pickwick Papers	With 8 Illustrations		....	0	3	6
Martin Chuzzlewit	With 8	„	....	0	3	6
Dombey and Son	With 8	„	....	0	3	6
Nicholas Nickleby	With 8	„	....	0	3	6
David Copperfield	With 8	„	....	0	3	6
Bleak House	With 8	„	....	0	3	6
Little Dorrit	With 8	„	....	0	3	6
Our Mutual Friend	With 8	„	....	0	3	6
Barnaby Rudge	With 8	„	....	0	3	6
Old Curiosity Shop	With 8	„	....	0	3	6
Tale of Two Cities	With 8	„	....	0	3	0
Sketches by Boz	With 8	„	....	0	3	0
American Notes, *and* Reprinted Pieces	With 8	„	....	0	3	0
Christmas Books	With 8	„	....	0	3	0
Oliver Twist	With 8	„	....	0	3	0
Great Expectations	With 8	„	....	0	3	0
Hard Times *and* Pictures from Italy	With 8	„	....	0	3	0
Uncommercial Traveller	With 4	„	....	0	3	0
A Child's History of England	With 4	„	....	0	3	6

DICKENS — THE LIFE OF CHARLES DICKENS. By John Forster. Vol. I., 1812-42. With Portraits and other Illustrations. 11th Edition. 8vo, cloth, 12s. Vol. II., 1842-52. 8vo, cloth, 14s. Vol. III. in the Press.

CHARLES DICKENS'S WORKS—*continued.*

HOUSEHOLD EDITION.

Now in course of publication in Weekly Numbers at 1*d.*, and in Monthly Parts at 6*d.*

Each penny number contains two new Illustrations.

OLIVER TWIST, with 28 Illustrations. Crown 4to, sewed, 1*s.* 6*d.*; in cloth, 2*s.* 6*d.*
MARTIN CHUZZLEWIT, with 59 Illustrations. Sewed, 3*s.*; in cloth, 4*s.*
DAVID COPPERFIELD, with 60 Illustrations and a Portrait. Sewed, 3*s.*, cloth, 4*s.*
BLEAK HOUSE. In course of publication.

MR. DICKENS'S READINGS.

Fcap. 8vo, sewed.

	s.	*d.*		*s.*	*d.*
Christmas Carol in Prose ..	1	0	Story of Little Dombey	1	0
Cricket on the Hearth	1	0	Poor Traveller, Boots at the Holly-Tree Inn, & Mrs. Gamp	1	0
Chimes: A Goblin Story	1	0			

DYCE'S SHAKESPEARE. New Edition, in Nine Volumes, demy 8vo. THE WORKS OF SHAKESPEARE. Edited by the Rev. Alexander Dyce. This edition is not a mere reprint of that which appeared in 1857, but presents a text very materially altered and amended from beginning to end, with a large body of critical Notes almost entirely new, and a Glossary, in which the language of the poet, his allusions to customs, &c., are fully explained. 9 vols., demy 8vo, 4*l.* 4*s.*

"The best text of Shakespeare which has yet appeared..... Mr. Dyce's Edition is a great work, worthy of his reputation, and for the present it contains the standard text."—*Times.*

DYCE (WILLIAM), R.A.—DRAWING-BOOK OF THE GOVERNMENT SCHOOL OF DESIGN, OR ELEMENTARY OUTLINES OF ORNAMENT. Fifty selected Plates, folio, sewed, 5*s.*

EARLE'S (J. C.) ENGLISH PREMIERS, FROM SIR ROBERT WALPOLE TO SIR ROBERT PEEL. 2 vols. Post 8vo, cloth, 21*s.*

ELEMENTARY DRAWING-BOOK. Directions for Introducing the First Steps of Elementary Drawing in Schools and among Workmen. Small 4to, cloth, 4*s.* 6*d.*

ELEMENTARY DRAWING COPY-BOOKS, for the Use of Children from four years old and upwards, in Schools and Families. Compiled by a Student certificated by the Science and Art Department as An Art Teacher. Three Books in 4to, sewed:—

Book 1. Letters, 1*s.*
,, 2. Geometrical and Ornamental Forms and Objects, 1*s.*
,, 3. Leaves, Flowers, Sprays, &c., 1*s.* 6*d.*

ELIOT (SIR JOHN)—A BIOGRAPHY BY JOHN FORSTER. *With Portraits. A new and cheaper edition.* 2 vols. Post 8vo, cloth, 14*s.*

ELLIOT'S (ROBERT H.) EXPERIENCES OF A PLANTER IN THE JUNGLES OF MYSORE. *With Illustrations and a Map.* 2 vols, 8vo, cloth, 24s.

—— CONCERNING JOHN'S INDIAN AFFAIRS. 8vo, cloth, 9s.

ELLIOT (FRANCES)—OLD COURT LIFE IN FRANCE. 2 vols. Demy 8vo. cloth. [*In the press.*

—— THE DIARY OF AN IDLE WOMAN IN ITALY. Second edition. Post 8vo, cloth, 6s.

—— PICTURES OF OLD ROME. New Edition, post 8vo, cloth, 6s.

FIGUIER (L.)—THE HUMAN RACE. Illustrated with 243 Wood Engravings and Eight Chromo Lithographs. Demy 8vo, cloth, 18s.

FINLAISON (ALEXANDER GLEN)—NEW GOVERNMENT SUCCESSION-DUTY TABLES. Third edition. Post 8vo, cloth, 5s.

FLEMING (GEORGE)—ANIMAL PLAGUES, THEIR HISTORY, NATURE, AND PREVENTION. 8vo, cloth, 15s.

—— RABIES AND HYDROPHOBIA; THEIR HISTORY, NATURE, CAUSES, SYMPTOMS, AND PREVENTION. With 8 Illustrations. 8vo, cloth, 15s.

—— HORSES AND HORSE-SHOEING; their Origin, History, Uses and Abuses. 210 Engravings. 8vo, cloth, 1*l*. 1s.

—— PRACTICAL HORSE-SHOEING. With 29 Illustrations. 8vo, sewed, 2s.

FORSTER (JOHN)—OLIVER GOLDSMITH: a Biography. With Illustrations. In 2 vols. Large crown 8vo, 21s.

———— WALTER SAVAGE LANDOR. A Biography. 1775-1864. With Portraits and Vignettes. 2 vols. Post 8vo, 1*l*. 8s.

———— SIR JOHN ELIOT: a Biography. *With Portraits. New and cheaper edition.* 2 vols. Post 8vo, cloth, 14s.

———— LIFE OF CHARLES DICKENS. Vol. I., 1812-42. With Portraits and other Illustrations. Eleventh edition, 8vo, cloth, 12s.

———————————————— Vol. II., 1842-52. 8vo, cloth. 14s.

FORSYTH (CAPT.)—THE HIGHLANDS OF CENTRAL INDIA. Notes on their Forests and Wild Tribes, Natural History and Sports. *With Map and Coloured Illustrations. Second Edition.* 8vo, cloth, 18s.

FORTNIGHTLY REVIEW.—First Series, May, 1865, to Dec. 1866. 6 vols, cloth, 13s. each.

———————————— New Series, 1867 to Present Time. In Half-yearly Volumes. Cloth, 13s. each.

FRANCATELLI (C. E.)—ROYAL CONFECTIONER; English and Foreign. A Practical Treatise. With Coloured Illustrations. New edition, post 8vo, cloth. [*Reprinting.*

FULLERTON (GEORGE)—FAMILY MEDICAL GUIDE. With plain Directions for the Treatment of every Case, and a List of Medicines required for any Household. 8vo, cloth, 12*s*.

FURLEY (JOHN)—STRUGGLES AND EXPERIENCES OF A NEUTRAL VOLUNTEER. With Maps. 2 vols. Post 8vo, cloth, 24*s*.

GERMAN NATIONAL COOKERY FOR ENGLISH KITCHENS. With Practical Descriptions of the Art of Cookery as performed in Germany, including small Pastry and Confectionary, Preserving, Pickling, and making of Vinegars, Liqueurs, and Beverages, warm and cold, also the Manufacture of the various German Sausages. Post 8vo, cloth.

GILLMORE PARKER ("UBIQUE")—ALL ROUND THE WORLD. Adventures in Europe, Asia, Africa, and America. With Illustrations by SYDNEY P. HALL. Post 8vo, cloth gilt, 7*s*. 6*d*.

GLEIG'S (LT.-COL. C. S. E.) THE OLD COLONEL AND THE OLD CORPS; with a View of Military Estates. Second Edition. Post 8vo, cloth, 6*s*.

HAKE (THOS. GORDON)—MADELINE, WITH OTHER POEMS AND PARABLES. Post 8vo, cloth, 7*s*. 6*d*.

——— PARABLES AND TALES. With Illustrations by ARTHUR HUGHES. Post 8vo, cloth.

HALL (SIDNEY)—A TRAVELLING ATLAS OF THE ENGLISH COUNTIES. Fifty Maps, coloured. New edition, including the railways, demy 8vo, in roan tuck, 10*s*. 6*d*.

HARDY (CAPT. C.)—FOREST LIFE IN ACADIE; and Sketches of Sport and Natural History in the Lower Provinces of the Canadian Dominion. With Illustrations. 8vo, cloth, 18*s*.

HAREM LIFE—THIRTY YEARS IN THE HAREM, OR LIFE IN TURKEY. By MADAME KIBRIZLI-MEHEMET-PASHA. 8vo, cloth, 14*s*.

HAWKINS (B. W.)—COMPARATIVE VIEW OF THE HUMAN AND ANIMAL FRAME. Small folio, cloth, 12*s*.

HOLBEIN (HANS)—LIFE. By R. N. WORNUM. With Portrait and Illustrations. Imp. 8vo, cloth, 31*s*. 6*d*.

HULME (F. E.)—A Series of 60 Outline Examples of Free-hand Ornament. Royal 8vo, sewed, 5*s*.

HUMPHRIS (H. D.)—PRINCIPLES OF PERSPECTIVE. Illustrated in a Series of Examples. Oblong folio, half bound, and Text 8vo, cloth, 21*s*.

HUTCHINSON (CAPT. ALEX. H.)—TRY CRACOW AND THE CARPATHIANS. With Map and Illustrations. Post 8vo, cloth, 8s.

——— TRY LAPLAND; a Fresh Field for Summer Tourists, with Illustrations and Map. Second Edition. Crown 8vo, cloth, 6s.

JEPHSON AND ELMHIRST.—OUR LIFE IN JAPAN. By R. MOUNTENEY JEPHSON, and E. PENNELL ELMHIRST, 9th Regt. With numerous Illustrations from Photographs by Lord WALTER KERR, Signor BEATO, and native Japanese Drawings. 8vo, cloth, 18s.

JUKES (J. BEETE)—LETTERS, AND EXTRACTS FROM HIS LETTERS AND OCCASIONAL WRITINGS. Edited with Memorial Notes by his Sister. Portrait. Post 8vo, cloth, 12s.

KEBBEL (T. E.)—THE AGRICULTURAL LABOURER. A Short Survey of his Position. Crown 8vo, 6s.

KENT (CHARLES)—CHARLES DICKENS AS A READER. Post 8vo, cloth, 8s.

KERAMIC GALLERY. Comprising upwards of 500 Illustrations of rare, curious, and choice examples of Pottery and Porcelain, from the Earliest Times to the Present, selected by the Author from the British Museum, the South Kensington Museum, the Geological Museum, and various Private Collections. With Historical Notices and Descriptions. By WILLIAM CHAFFERS. Two handsome Vols. Royal 8vo. Price 4*l*. 4*s*.

KONINCK (L. L. DE), AND DIETZ (E.)—PRACTICAL MANUAL OF CHEMICAL ASSAYING, as applied to the Manufacture of Iron from its Ores, and to Cast Iron, Wrought Iron, and Steel, as found in Commerce. Edited, with Notes, by ROBERT MALLET. Post 8vo, cloth.

LACORDAIRE (PÈRE)—JESUS CHRIST. Conferences delivered at Notre Dame in Paris. Translated, with the Author's permission, by a Tertiary of the same order. Crown 8vo, cloth, 6s.

——— GOD. Conferences delivered at Notre Dame, in Paris. By the same Translator. Crown 8vo, cloth, 6s.

——— GOD AND MAN. A Third Volume by the same Translator. Crown 8vo, cloth, 6s.

LACROIX (P.)—THE MANNERS, CUSTOMS, AND COSTUMES OF THE MIDDLE AGES. With 15 Chromo-lithographs and 440 Wood Engravings. Royal 8vo. [*In the press.*

——— THE ARTS OF THE MIDDLE AGES, AND AT THE PERIOD OF THE RENAISSANCE. With 19 Chromo-lithographs and over 400 Woodcuts. Royal 8vo, half morocco, 31*s*. 6*d*.

LANDOR'S (WALTER SAVAGE) WORKS. 2 vols., royal 8vo, cloth, 21*s.*

——————————— **A BIOGRAPHY.** 1775-1864. By JOHN FORSTER. Portraits and Vignettes. 2 vols., post 8vo, 1*l.* 8*s.*

LEROY (CHARLES GEORGES)—THE INTELLIGENCE AND PERFECTIBILITY OF ANIMALS, from a Philosophic Point of View, with a few Letters on Man. Post 8vo, cloth, 7*s.* 6*d.*

LEVER'S (CHARLES) WORKS.

THE ORIGINAL EDITION WITH THE ILLUSTRATIONS.

In demy 8vo Volumes, cloth, 6s. each.

DAVENPORT DUNN.
TOM BURKE OF OURS.
HARRY LORREQUER.
JACK HINTON.
ONE OF THEM.
CHARLES O'MALLEY.
THE O'DONOGHUE.
BARRINGTON.
DODD FAMILY ABROAD.
KNIGHT OF GWYNNE.
LUTTRELL OF ARRAN.
BRAMLEIGHS OF BISHOP BRAMLEIGH.
THE DALTONS.
MARTINS OF CROMARTIN.
ROLAND CASHEL.

LEVER'S (CHARLES) WORKS.—CHEAP EDITION.

Fancy boards, 3s., or cloth, 3s. 6d. each.

CHARLES O'MALLEY.
TOM BURKE.
THE KNIGHT OF GWYNNE.

Fancy boards, s. 6d., or cloth, 3s. 6d. each.

MARTINS OF CROMARTIN.
THE DALTONS.
ROLAND CASHEL.
DAVENPORT DUNN.
DODD FAMILY.
MAURICE TIERNAY.
SIR BROOKE FOSBROOKE.

Fancy boards, 2s., or cloth, 3s. each.

THE O'DONOGHUE.
FORTUNES OF GLENCORE.
HARRY LORREQUER.
ONE OF THEM.
SIR JASPER CAREW.
A DAY'S RIDE.
JACK HINTON.
BARRINGTON.
LUTTRELL OF ARRAN.
RENT IN THE CLOUD and ST. PATRICK'S EVE.
CON CREGAN.
ARTHUR O'LEARY.

Or in sets of 21 Vols., cloth, for £3 3s.

LEVY'S (W. HANKS) BLINDNESS AND THE BLIND; or a Treatise on the Science of Typhology. Post 8vo, cloth, 7*s.* 6*d.*

LYTTON (HON. ROBT.)—"OWEN MEREDITH."—ORVAL; or the Fool of Time, and other Imitations and Paraphrases. 12mo, cloth, 9s.

—— CHRONICLES AND CHARACTERS. With Portrait. 2 vols., crown 8vo, cloth, 1*l*. 4*s*.

—— POETICAL WORKS—COLLECTED EDITION.

Vol. I.—CLYTEMNESTRA, and Poems Lyrical and Descriptive. 12mo, cloth. *Reprinting*.
,, II.—LUCILE. 12mo, cloth, 6*s*.

—— SERBSKI PESME; or, National Songs of Servia. Fcap. cloth, 4*s*.

LYTTON (LORD)—MONEY. A Comedy. Demy 8vo, sewed, 2*s*. 6*d*.

—— NOT SO BAD AS WE SEEM. A Comedy. Demy 8vo, sewed, 2*s*. 6*d*.

—— RICHELIEU; OR, THE CONSPIRACY. A Play. Demy 8vo, sewed, 2*s*. 6*d*.

—— LADY OF LYONS, OR LOVE AND PRIDE. A Play. Demy 8vo, sewed, 2*s*. 6*d*.

MALLET (DR. J. W.)—COTTON: THE CHEMICAL, &c., CONDITIONS OF ITS SUCCESSFUL CULTIVATION. Post 8vo, cloth, 7*s*. 6*d*.

MALLET (ROBERT)—GREAT NEAPOLITAN EARTHQUAKE OF 1857. First Principles of Observational Seismology: as developed in the Report to the Royal Society of London, of the Expedition made into the Interior of the Kingdom of Naples, to investigate the Circumstances of the great Earthquake of December, 1857. Maps and numerous Illustrations. 2 vols., royal 8vo, cloth, 63*s*.

MARTINDALE (LT.-COL. C.B.)—RECOLLECTIONS OF CANADA. With numerous Illustrations by Lieut. CARLILE.

MELEK-HANUM (WIFE OF H.H. KIBRIZLI-MEHEMET-PASHA)—THIRTY YEARS IN THE HAREM. An Autobiography. 8vo, cloth, 14*s*.

MELVILLE (G. J. WHYTE)—SATANELLA, A STORY ON PUNCHESTOWN. With Illustrations. 2 Vols. Post 8vo, cloth, 21*s*.

WHYTE-MELVILLE'S WORKS.—CHEAP EDITION.

Crown 8vo, fancy boards, 2s. each, or 2s. 6d. in cloth.

THE WHITE ROSE.
CERISE. A Tale of the Last Century.
BROOKES OF BRIDLEMERE.
"BONES AND I;" or, The Skeleton at Home.
"M., OR N." Similia Similibus Curantur.
CONTRABAND, OR A LOSING HAZARD.
MARKET HARBOROUGH; or, How Mr. Sawyer went to the Shires.
SARCHEDON, A LEGEND OF THE GREAT QUEEN.
SONGS AND VERSES.

MEREDITH (GEORGE)—SHAVING OF SHAGPAT. An Arabian Entertainment. Crown 8vo, fancy boards, 2*s*.

—— MODERN LOVE, AND POEMS OF THE ENGLISH ROADSIDE, with Poems and Ballads. Fcap, cloth, 6*s*.

MILTON'S (JOHN) LIFE, OPINOINS, AND WRITINGS. With an Introduction to "Paradise Lost," by THOMAS KEIGHTLEY, 8vo, cloth, 10*s*. 6*d*.

MOLESWORTH (W. NASSAU)—HISTORY OF ENGLAND FROM THE YEAR 1830. Vols. I. and II. 8vo, cloth, each 15*s*.

—————— Vol. III. *In the press.*

MORLEY (HENRY)—ENGLISH WRITERS. To be completed in 3 Vols. Part I. Vol. I. THE CELTS AND ANGLO-SAXONS. With an Introductory Sketch of the Four Periods of English Literature. Part 2. FROM THE CONQUEST TO CHAUCER. (Making 2 vols.) 8vo, cloth, 22*s*.

*** Each Part is indexed separately. The Two Parts complete the account of English Literature during the Period of the Formation of the Language, or of THE WRITERS BEFORE CHAUCER.

—— Vol. II. Part I. FROM CHAUCER TO DUNBAR. 8vo, cloth, 12*s*.

—— TABLES OF ENGLISH LITERATURE. Containing 20 Charts. Second edition, with Index. Royal 4to, cloth, 12*s*.

In Three Parts. Parts I. and II., containing Three Charts, each 1*s*. 6*d*.

Part III. containing 14 Charts, 7*s*. Part III. also kept in Sections, 1, 2, and 5, 1*s*. 6*d*. each; 3 and 4 together, 3*s*. *** *The Charts sold separately.*

—— CLEMENT MAROT AND OTHER STUDIES. 2 Vols. Post 8vo, cloth, 18*s*.

MORLEY (JOHN)—ROUSSEAU. 2 vols., 8vo, cloth. [*In the press.*

—— VOLTAIRE. Cheap Edition. Crown 8vo. 6*s*.

—— CRITICAL MISCELLANIES. 8vo, cloth, 14*s*.

NAPIER (C. O. GROOM)—TOMMY TRY, AND WHAT HE DID IN SCIENCE. A Book for Boys. With 46 Illustrations. Crown 8vo, 6*s*.

NAPIER (MAJ.-GEN. W. C. E.)—OUTPOST DUTY. By General JARRY, translated with TREATISES ON MILITARY RECONNAISSANCE AND ON ROAD-MAKING. Second edition. Crown 8vo, 5*s*.

OUR FARM OF FOUR ACRES. How we Managed it, the Money we Made by it, and How it Grew to one of Six Acres. 5th Enlarged and Illustrated Edition. Post 8vo, cloth, 2*s*. 6*d*.

OUIDA—A DOG OF FLANDERS AND OTHER STORIES. With 4 Illustrations. Demy 8vo, cloth, 10*s*. 6*d*.

OUIDA'S NOVELS.

Cheap Editions.

FOLLE-FARINE. Crown 8vo, 5*s*.

IDALIA. Crown 8vo, 5*s*.

CHANDOS. Crown 8vo, 5*s*.

UNDER TWO FLAGS. Crown 8vo, 5*s*.

CECIL CASTLEMAINE'S GAGE. Crown 8vo, 5*s*.

TRICOTRIN; The Story of a Waif and Stray. Crown 8vo, 5*s*.

STRATHMORE, or Wrought by his Own Hand. Crown 8vo, 5*s*.

HELD IN BONDAGE, or Granville de Vigne. Crown 8vo, 5*s*.

PUCK. His Vicissitudes, Adventures, &c. Crown 8vo, 5*s*.

PIM (B.) and SEEMANN (B.)—DOTTINGS ON THE ROADSIDE IN PANAMA, NICARAGUA, AND MOSQUITO. With Plates and Maps. 8vo, cloth, 18*s*.

PUCKETT, R. CAMPBELL (Head Master of the Bath School of Art)—SCIOGRAPHY; or Radial Projection of Shadows. New Edition. Crown 8vo, cloth, 6*s*.

RECLUS (ÉLISÉE)—THE EARTH. A Descriptive History of the Phenomena of the Life of the Globe. Sections 1 and 2, Continents. Translated by the late B. B. Woodward, M.A., and Edited by Henry Woodward, British Museum. Illustrated by 230 Maps inserted in the text, and 24 page Maps printed in Colours. 2 vols. 8vo, cloth, 26*s*.

—— THE OCEAN, ATMOSPHERE, AND LIFE. Being the Second Series of a Descriptive History of the Life of the Globe. Illustrated with 250 Maps or Figures, and 27 Maps printed in colours. 2 Vols. 8vo, cloth, 26*s*.

RALEIGH, LIFE OF SIR WALTER, 1552-1618. By J. A. St. John. New edition, post 8vo, 10*s*. 6*d*.

RECORDS OF THE KING'S OWN BORDERERS, or Old Edinburgh Regiment. 8vo, cloth, 14*s*.

REDGRAVE (RICHARD)—MANUAL AND CATECHISM ON COLOUR. 24mo, cloth, 9*d*.

REYNOLDS (REV. R. VINCENT)—THE CHURCH AND THE PEOPLE; or, The Adaptation of the Church's Machinery to the Exigencies of the Times. Post 8vo, 6*s*.

RIDGE (DR. BENJAMIN)—OURSELVES, OUR FOOD, AND OUR PHYSIC. Twelfth Edition, fcap 8vo, cloth, 1*s*. 6*d*.

ROBERTS (SIR RANDAL, BART.)—GLENMAHRA; or the Western Highlands, with Illustrations. Crown 8vo, 6*s*.

—— MODERN WAR; or the Campaign of the First Prussian Army, 1870—1871. With Map. 8vo, cloth. 14*s*.

ROBINSON (J. C.)—ITALIAN SCULPTURE OF THE MIDDLE AGES AND PERIOD OF THE REVIVAL OF ART. A Descriptive Catalogue of that section of the South Kensington Museum comprising an Account of the Acquisitions from the Gigli and Campana Collections. With Twenty Engravings. Royal 8vo, cloth, 7*s*. 6*d*.

ROCK (DR.)—ON TEXTILE FABRICS. A Descriptive Catalogue of the Collection of Church Vestments, Dresses, Silk Stuffs, Needlework and Tapestries in the South Kensington Museum. By the Very Rev. Canon ROCK, D.D. Royal 8vo, half morocco, 31*s*. 6*d*.

ROME. By FRANCIS WEY. With an Introduction by W. W. STORY, Author of "Roba di Roma." Containing 345 beautiful Illustrations. Forming a magnificent volume in super royal 4to, cloth, £3.

ROSSEL'S POSTHUMOUS PAPERS. Translated from the French. Post 8vo, cloth, 8*s*.

SARCEY (FRANCISQUE)—PARIS DURING THE SIEGE. *Translated from the French. With a Map.* Post 8vo, cloth, 6*s*. 6*d*.

SHAFTESBURY (EARL OF) — SPEECHES UPON SUBJECTS HAVING RELATION CHIEFLY TO THE CLAIMS AND INTERESTS OF THE LABOURING CLASS. With a Preface. Crown 8vo, 8*s*.

SHAIRP (THOMAS)—UP IN THE NORTH; Notes of a Journey from London to Lulea and into Lapland. With Map and Illustrations. Post 8vo, cloth, 8*s*.

SHAKESPEARE (DYCE'S). New Edition, in Nine Volumes, demy 8vo. —THE WORKS OF SHAKESPEARE. Edited by the Rev. ALEXANDER DYCE. This edition is not a mere reprint of that which appeared in 1857, but presents a text very materially altered and amended from beginning to end, with a large body of critical Notes almost entirely new, and a Glossary, in which the language of the poet, his allusions to customs, &c., are fully explained. 9 vols., demy 8vo, cloth, 4*l*. 4*s*.

"The best text of Shakespeare which has yet appeared. . . . . . Mr. Dyce's Edition is a great work, worthy of his reputation, and for the present it contains the standard text."—*Times*.

SIMONIN (L.) — UNDERGROUND LIFE; or Mines and Miners. Translated, Adapted to the Present State of British Mining, and Edited by H. W. Bristowe, F.R.S., of the Geological Survey, &c. With 160 Engravings on Wood, 20 Maps Geologically coloured, and 10 Plates of Metals and Minerals printed in Chromo-lithography. Imperial 8vo. Roxburghe binding, 42*s*.

SMITH (SAMUEL, of Woodberry Down)—LYRICS OF A LIFE TIME. With Illustrations. Post 8vo, cloth, 8*s*.

STORY (W. W.)—ROBA DI ROMA. Sixth Edition, with Additions and Portrait. Post 8vo, cloth, 10*s*. 6*d*.

—— THE PROPORTIONS OF THE HUMAN FRAME, ACCORDING TO A NEW CANON. With Plates. Royal 8vo, cloth, 10*s*.

STUDIES IN CONDUCT. Short Essays from the "Saturday Review." Post 8vo, cloth, 7*s.* 6*d.*

TAINSH (E. C.) — A STUDY OF THE WORKS OF ALFRED TENNYSON, D.C.L., POET LAUREATE. New edition, with Supplementary Chapter on the "HOLY GRAIL." Crown 8vo, cloth, 6*s.*

THIRTY YEARS IN THE HAREM; or Life in Turkey. By Mad. KIBRIZLI-MEHEMET-PASHA. 8vo, cloth, 14*s.*

TRINAL—MEMORIALS OF THEOPHILUS TRINAL, STUDENT. By the Rev. T. T. LYNCH. New Edition, enlarged. Crown 8vo, cloth extra, 6*s.*

TROLLOPE (ANTHONY)—THE EUSTACE DIAMONDS. 3 Vols. Post 8vo, cloth, 31*s.* 6*d.*

HUNTING SKETCHES. Cloth, 3*s.* 6*d.*
TRAVELLING SKETCHES. Cloth, 3*s.* 6*d.*
CLERGYMEN OF THE CHURCH OF ENGLAND. 3*s.* 6*d.*
THE BELTON ESTATE. 5*s.*

TROLLOPE'S (ANTHONY) NOVELS.—CHEAP EDITIONS.

Boards, 3s., cloth, 3s. 6d.

PHINEAS FINN.
CAN YOU FORGIVE HER.

Boards, 2s. 6d., cloth, 3s. 6d.

ORLEY FARM.
DOCTOR THORNE.
HE KNEW HE WAS RIGHT.
RALPH THE HEIR.
THE BERTRAMS.

Boards, 2s., cloth, 3s.

KELLYS AND O'KELLYS.
McDERMOT OF BALLYCLORAN.
CASTLE RICHMOND.
BELTON ESTATE.
MISS MACKENSIE.
RACHEL RAY.
TALES OF ALL COUNTRIES.
MARY GRESLEY.
LOTTA SCHMIDT.

TROLLOPE (THOMAS ADOLPHUS)—A HISTORY OF THE COMMONWEALTH OF FLORENCE. From the Earliest Independence of the Commune to the Fall of the Republic in 1531. 4 vols., demy 8vo, cloth, £3.

TURNOR (HATTON)—ASTRA CASTA. Experiments and Adventures in the Atmosphere. With upwards of 100 Engravings and Photozinco-graphic Plates produced under the superintendence of Colonel Sir HENRY JAMES, R.E. Second Edition. Royal 4to, cloth, 35*s.*

UNIVERSAL CATALOGUE OF BOOKS ON ART. Compiled for the use of the National Art Library, and the Schools of Art in the United Kingdom. In 2 vols., crown 4to, half morocco, 21*s.* each.

VERNE (JULES)—FIVE WEEKS IN A BALLOON. A Voyage of Exploration and Discovery in Central Africa. Translated from the French. With 64 Illustrations. Post 8vo, 7*s.* 6*d.*

VÉSINIER, P. (Ex-Member and Secretary of the Commune, and Rédacteur en chef du Journal Officiel)—HISTORY OF THE COMMUNE OF PARIS. Post 8vo, cloth, 7*s.* 6*d.*

VOLTAIRE. By JOHN MORLEY. Cheap Edition. Crown 8vo. 6*s.*

WEY (FRANCIS)—ROME. By FRANCIS WEY. With an Introduction by W. W. STORY, Author of "Roba di Roma." Containing 345 beautiful Illustrations. Forming a magnificent volume in super royal 4to, cloth, £3.

WHIST PLAYER (THE). By Colonel BLYTH. With Coloured Plates of "Hands." Third Edition. Imperial 16mo, cloth, 5*s.*

WHITE (WALTER)—EASTERN ENGLAND. From the Thames to the Humber. 2 vols., post 8vo, cloth, 18*s.*

——— MONTH IN YORKSHIRE. Fourth Edition. With a Map. Post 8vo, cloth, 4*s.*

——— LONDONER'S WALK TO THE LAND'S END, AND A TRIP TO THE SCILLY ISLES. With Four Maps. Second Edition. Post 8vo, 4*s.*

WORNUM (R. N.)—THE EPOCHS OF PAINTING. A Biographical and Critical Essay on Painting and Painters of all Times and many Places. With numerous Illustrations. Demy 8vo, cloth, 20*s.*

——— ANALYSIS OF ORNAMENT—THE CHARACTERISTICS OF STYLES. An Introduction to the Study of the History of Ornamental Art. *With many Illustrations.* Second Edition. Royal 8vo, cloth, 8*s.*

——— THE LIFE OF HOLBEIN, PAINTER OF AUGSBURG. With Portrait and 34 Illustrations. Imperial 8vo, cloth, 31*s.* 6*d.*

WYNTER (DR.)—CURIOSITIES OF TOIL, AND OTHER PAPERS. 2 vols, post 8vo, 18*s.*

YONGE (C. D.)—PARALLEL LIVES OF ANCIENT AND MODERN HEROES. New Edition. 12mo, cloth, 4*s.* 6*d.*

BOOKS FOR THE USE OF SCHOOLS.

Issued under the Authority of the Science and Art Department, South Kensington.

AN ALPHABET OF COLOUR. Reduced from the works of FIELD, HAY, CHEVREUIL. 4to, sewed, 3*s.*

ART DIRECTORY. 12mo, sewed, 6*d.*

BRADLEY (THOMAS), of the Royal Military Academy, Woolwich—ELEMENTS OF GEOMETRICAL DRAWING. In Two Parts, with Sixty Plates, oblong folio, half-bound, each part, 16*s.*

—— Selection (from the above) of Twenty Plates, for the use of the Royal Military Academy, Woolwich. Oblong folio, half-bound, 10*s.*

BURCHETT'S LINEAR PERSPECTIVE. With Illustrations. Post 8vo, cloth, 7*s.*

—— PRACTICAL GEOMETRY. Post 8vo, cloth, 5*s.*

—— DEFINITIONS OF GEOMETRY. Third Edition, 24mo, sewed, 5*d.*

DAVIDSON (ELLIS A.)—DRAWING FOR ELEMENTARY SCHOOLS. Post 8vo, cloth, 3*s.*

—— ORTHOGRAPHIC AND ISOMETRICAL PROJECTION. 12mo, cloth, 2*s.*

—— LINEAR DRAWING. Geometry applied to Trade and Manufactures. 12mo, cloth, 2*s.*

—— DRAWING FOR CARPENTERS AND JOINERS. 12mo, cloth, 3*s.* 6*d.*

—— BUILDING, CONSTRUCTION, AND ARCHITECTURAL DRAWING. 12mo, cloth, 2*s.*

—— MODEL DRAWING. 12mo, cloth, 3*s.*

—— PRACTICAL PERSPECTIVE. 12mo, cloth, 3*s.*

DELAMOTTE (P. H.)—PROGRESSIVE DRAWING BOOK FOR BEGINNERS. 12mo, 2*s.* 6*d.*

DICKSEE (J. R.)—SCHOOL PERSPECTIVE. 8vo, cloth, 4*s.* 6*d.*

DIRECTIONS FOR INTRODUCING ELEMENTARY DRAWING IN SCHOOLS AND AMONG WORKMEN. Published at the Request of the Society of Arts. Small 4to, cloth, 4*s.* 6*d.*

DRAWING FOR YOUNG CHILDREN, 150 Copies. 16mo, cloth, 3*s.* 6*d.*

DYCE'S DRAWING BOOK OF THE GOVERNMENT SCHOOL OF DESIGN, ELEMENTARY OUTLINES OF ORNAMENT. 50 Plates, small folio, sewed, 5*s*.

——— Introduction to ditto. Foolscap 8vo, 6*d*.

EDUCATIONAL DIVISION OF S. K. MUSEUM. Classified Catalogue of, 8vo, *reprinting*.

ELEMENTARY DRAWING COPY-BOOKS, for the use of Children from four years old and upwards, in Schools and Families. Compiled by a Student certificated by the Science and Art Department as an ART TEACHER. Seven Books in 4to. sewed:—

Book I. Letters, 8*d*.
" II. Ditto, 8*d*.
" III. Geometrical and Ornamental Forms, 8*d*.
" IV. Objects, 8*d*.
" V. Leaves, 8*d*.
" VI. Birds, Animals, &c., 8*d*.
" VII. Leaves, Flowers, and Sprays, 8*d*.

. Or in Sets of Seven Books, 4*s*. 6*d*.

ENGINEER AND MACHINIST DRAWING BOOK, 16 parts, 71 plates, folio, 32*s*.

ditto " " ditto " 15 by 12 in., mounted, 64*s*.

EXAMINATION PAPERS FOR SCIENCE SCHOOLS AND CLASSES. [*Annual.*]

FOSTER (VERE)—DRAWING COPY BOOKS. Fcap. 4to, 1*d*. each.

ditto " " fine paper with additions, fcap. 4to, 3*d*. each.

GREGORY (CHAS.)—FIRST GRADE FREEHAND OUTLINE DRAWING EXAMPLES (for the black board), 4to, packet, 2*s*. 6*d*.

HENSLOW (PROF.)—ILLUSTRATIONS TO BE EMPLOYED IN THE PRACTICAL LESSONS ON BOTANY. Prepared for South Kensington Museum. Post 8vo, sewed, 6*d*.

HULME (F. E.)—SIXTY OUTLINE EXAMPLES OF FREEHAND ORNAMENT. Royal 8vo, sewed, 5*s*.

JEWITT'S HANDBOOK OF PRACTICAL PERSPECTIVE. 18mo, cloth, 1*s*. 6*d*.

KENNEDY (JOHN)—FIRST GRADE PRACTICAL GEOMETRY, 12mo, 6*d*.

——— FREEHAND DRAWING BOOK, 16mo, cloth, 1*s*. 6*d*.

LAXTON'S EXAMPLES OF BUILDING CONSTRUCTION, 1 and 2 divisions, folio, each containing 16 plates, 10*s*. each.

LINDLEY (JOHN)—SYMMETRY OF VEGETATION, principles to be observed in the delineation of plants. 12mo, sewed, 1*s*.

MARSHALL'S HUMAN BODY. Text and Plates, 2 vols., cloth, 21*s*.

PRINCIPLES OF DECORATIVE ART. Folio, sewed, 1*s.*

PUCKETT, R. CAMPBELL (Head Master of the Bath School of Art)—
SCIOGRAPHY OR RADIAL PROJECTION OF SHADOWS. Crown 8vo, cloth, 6*s.*

REDGRAVE'S MANUAL AND CATECHISM ON COLOUR. Second Edition. 24mo, sewed, 9*d.*

ROBINSON'S (J. C.)—LECTURE ON THE MUSEUM OF ORNAMENTAL ART. Fcap. 8vo, sewed, 6*d.*

—— MANUAL OF ELEMENTARY OUTLINE DRAWING FOR THE COURSE OF FLAT EXAMPLES. 32mo, 7*d.*

SCIENCE DIRECTORY, 12mo, sewed, 6*d.*

WALLIS (GEORGE)—DRAWING BOOK, oblong, sewed, 3*s.* 6*d.*

ditto ,, ditto, mounted, 8*s.*

WORNUM (R. N.)—THE CHARACTERISTICS OF STYLES; An Introduction to the Study of the History of Ornamental Art. Royal 8vo, cloth, 8*s.*

—— CATALOGUE OF ORNAMENTAL CASTS. 8vo, cloth, 1*s.* 6*d.*

OUTLINE EXAMPLES.

A. O. S. LETTERS, 3 sheets, 1*s.*, mounted, 3*s.*

ALBERTOLLI, Selections of Foliage from, 4 plates, 5*d.*, mounted, 3*s.* 6*d.*

FAMILIAR OBJECTS. Mounted, 9*d.*

FLOWERS OUTLINED FROM THE FLAT. 8 sheets, 8*d.*, mounted, 3*s.* 0*d.*

MORGHEN'S OUTLINE OF HUMAN FIGURE. By HERMAN, 20 sheets, 3*s.* 4*d.*, mounted, 15*s.*

SIMPSON'S 12 OUTLINES FOR PENCIL DRAWING. Mounted, 7*s.*

TARSIA. Ornament Outlined from the Flat. Wood Mosaic, 4 plates, 7*d.*, mounted, 3*s.* 6*d.*

TRAJAN FRIEZE FROM THE FORUM OF TRAJAN, Part of a, 4*d.*, mounted, 1*s.*

WEITBRICHT'S OUTLINES OF ORNAMENT. By HERMAN, 12 sheets, 2*s.*, mounted, 8*s.* 6*d.*

DELARUE'S FLAT EXAMPLES FOR DRAWING, OBJECTS, 48 subjects, in packet, 5*s.*

—— —— —— —— ANIMALS, in packet, 1*s.*

DYCE'S ELEMENTARY OUTLINES OF ORNAMENT. Drawing Book of the Government School of Design, 50 plates, sewed, 5*s.*, mounted, 18*s.*

—— SELECTION OF 15 PLATES FROM DO. Mounted, 6*s.* 6*d.*

SMITH'S (W.) EXAMPLES OF FIRST PRACTICE IN FREEHAND OUTLINE DRAWING, Diagrams for the Black Board, packets, 2*s.*

WALLIS'S DRAWING BOOK. Oblong, sewed, 3*s.* 6*d.*, mounted, 8*s.*

SHADED EXAMPLES.

BARGUE'S COURSE OF DESIGN. 20 selected sheets, each sheet, 2*s*.

DORIC RENAISSANCE FRIEZE ORNAMENT (shaded ornament), sheet, 4*d*., mounted, 1*s*. 2*d*.

EARLY ENGLISH CAPITAL. Sheet, 4*d*., mounted, 1*s*.

GOTHIC PATERA. Sheet, 4*d*., mounted, 1*s*.

GREEK FRIEZE, FROM A. Sheet, 3*d*., mounted, 9*d*.

PILASTER, PART OF A. From the tomb of St. Biagio, at Pisa. Sheet, 1*s*., mounted, 2*s*.

RENAISSANCE SCROLL. Sheet, 6*d*., mounted, 1*s*. 4*d*.

RENAISSANCE ROSETTE. Sheet, 3*d*., mounted, 9*d*.

SCULPTURED FOLIAGE, DECORATED, MOULDING OF. Sheet, 7*d*., mounted, 1*s*. 2*d*.

COLUMN FROM THE VATICAN. Sheet 1*s*., mounted, 2*s*.

WHITE GRAPES. Sheet, 9*d*., mounted, 2*s*.

VIRGINIA CREEPER. Sheet, 9*d*., mounted, 2*s*.

BURDOCK. Sheet, 4*d*., mounted, 1*s*. 2*d*.

POPPY. Sheet, 4*d*., mounted, 1*s*. 2*d*.

FOLIATED SCROLL FROM THE VATICAN. Sheet 5*d*., mounted, 1*s*. 3*d*.

COLOURED EXAMPLES.

CAMELLIA. Sheet, 2*s*. 9*d*., mounted, 3*s*. 9*d*.

PELARGONIUM. Sheet, 2*s*. 9*d*., mounted, 3*s*. 9*d*.

PETUNIA. Sheet, 2*s*. 9*d*., mounted, 3*s*. 9*d*.

NASTURTIUM. Sheet, 2*s*. 9*d*., mounted, 3*s*. 9*d*.

OLEANDER. Sheet, 2*s*. 9*d*., mounted, 3*s*. 9*d*.

GROUP OF CAMELLIAS. Mounted, 12*s*.

DIAGRAM TO ILLUSTRATE THE HARMONIOUS RELATIONS OF COLOUR. Sheet, 9*d*., mounted, 1*s*. 6*d*.

ELEMENTARY DESIGN. 2 plates, sheet, 1*s*.

PYNE'S LANDSCAPES IN CHROMO-LITHOGRAPHY, (six) each, mounted, 7*s*. 6*d*.

COTMAN'S PENCIL LANDSCAPES, (nine) set, mounted, 15*s*.

—— SEPIA —— (five) set, mounted, 20*s*.

DOWNE CASTLE, CHROMO-LITHOGRAPH. Mounted, 7*s*.

PETIT (STANISLAS)—SELECTED EXAMPLES OF MACHINES OF IRON AND WOODWORK (FRENCH). 60 sheets, each 1*s*. 1*d*.

TRIPON (J. B.)—ARCHITECTURAL STUDIES. 20 plates, each 1*s*. 8*d*.

LINEAL DRAWING COPIES. In portfolio, 5*s*. 6*d*.

DESIGN OF AN AXMINSTER CARPET. By MARY JULYAN. 2*s*.

MODELS AND INSTRUMENTS.

A BOX OF MODELS FOR PAROCHIAL SCHOOLS. £1 4*s.*

BINN'S BOX OF MODELS FOR ORTHOGRAPHIC PROJECTION APPLIED TO MECHANICAL DRAWING. In a box, 30*s.*

DAVIDSON'S BOX OF DRAWING MODELS. 40*s.*

RIGG'S LARGE (WOOD) COMPASSES, WITH CHALK HOLDER. 4*s.* 3*d.*

SET OF LARGE MODELS. A Wire Quadrangle, with a Circle and Cross within it, and one Straight Wire. A Solid Cube. A Skeleton Wire Cube. A Sphere. A Cone. A Cylinder. A Hexagonal Prism. £2 2*s.*

MODELS OF BUILDING CONSTRUCTION. Details of a king-post truss. £2.

———— Details of a six-inch trussed partition for floor, £3 3*s.*

———— Details of a trussed timber beam for a traveller, £4 10*s.*

These models are constructed in wood and iron.

SKELETON CUBE IN WOOD. 3*s.* 6*d.*

A STAND WITH A UNIVERSAL JOINT, to Show the Solid Models, &c. £1 10*s.*

SLIP, TWO SET SQUARES, AND T-SQUARE. 5*s.*

SPECIMENS OF THE DRAWING-BOARD, T-SQUARE, COMPASSES, BOOKS ON GEOMETRY AND COLOUR, CASE OF PENCILS AND COLOUR-BOX; awarded to Students in Parish Schools. 13*s.* 6*d.*

IMPERIAL DEAL FRAMES, glazed, without sunk rings, 10*s.*

ELLIOTT'S CASE OF INSTRUMENTS. Containing 6-in. compasses with pen and pencil leg. 6*s.* 9*d.*

——— PRIZE INSTRUMENT CASE, with 6-in compasses, pen and pencil leg, two small compasses, pen and scale. 18*s.*

——— 6-IN COMPASSES, WITH SHIFTING PEN AND POINT, 4*s.*

THREE OBJECTS OF FORM IN POTTERY (MINTON'S)—INDIAN JAR; CELADON JAR; BOTTLE. 15*s.* 9*d.*

FIVE SELECTED VASES IN MAJOLICA WARE (MINTON'S). £2 11*s.*

THREE SELECTED VASES IN EARTHENWARE (WEDGWOOD'S), 15*s.* 6*d.*

LARGE DIAGRAMS.

ASTRONOMICAL. Twelve sheets. Prepared for the Committee of Council of Education by JOHN DREW, Ph. Dr., F.R.S.A., each sheet, 4s.

——— on rollers and varnished, each, 7s.

BUILDING CONSTRUCTION. By WILLIAM J. GLENNY, Professor of Drawing, King's College. 10 sheets. In sets, 21s.

PHYSIOLOGICAL. Nine sheets. Illustrating Human Physiology, Life-size and Coloured from Nature. Prepared under the direction of JOHN MARSHALL, M.R.C.S., each sheet, 12s. 6d.

1. SKELETON AND LIGAMENTS.
2. MUSCLES, JOINTS, &c.
3. VISCERA AND LUNGS.
4. HEART AND BLOOD VESSELS.
5. LYMPHATICS OR ABSORBENTS.
6. DIGESTIVE ORGANS.
7. BRAIN AND NERVES.
8. ORGANS OF THE SENSES.
9. TEXTURES, MICROSCOPIC STRUCTURE.

On canvas and rollers, varnished, each, 21s.

ZOOLOGICAL. Ten sheets. Illustrating the Classification of Animals. By ROBERT PATTERSON. Each sheet, 4s.

——— on canvas and rollers, varnished, each, 7s.

The same, reduced in size, on Royal paper, in nine sheets, uncoloured, 12s.

BOTANICAL. Nine sheets. Illustrating a Practical Method of Teaching Botany. By Professor HENSLOW, F.L.S. 40s.

——— on canvas and rollers, and varnished, £3 3s.

MECHANICAL. Six sheets. Pump, Hydraulic Press, Water Wheel, Turbine, Locomotive Engine, Stationary Engine, 62½-in. by 47-in., on canvas and roller, each 16s. 6d.

ILLUSTRATIONS OF THE PRINCIPAL NATURAL ORDERS OF THE VEGETABLE KINGDOM. By Professor OLIVER, F.R.S., F.L.S. Seventy Imperial sheets containing examples of dried plants, representing the different orders. Five guineas the set, in a box.

Bradbury Agnew, & Co.,] [Printers, Whitefriars, London.

www.ingramcontent.com/pod-product-compliance
Lightning Source LLC
Chambersburg PA
CBHW020504270326
41926CB00008B/734

* 9 7 8 3 7 4 3 3 2 2 2 5 7 *